A SCOTTISH WEDDING

Woo'ed an' married an' a'

An exploration of Scottish Wedding customs.

Gordon J. Mooney

Traditional Music Books, Lauder, Scotland, 1999

ISBN: 0 9533975 0 5

First Published in 1999

This edition published by
Traditional Music Books
4 The Avenue,
Lauder,
Berwickshire,
TD2 6TD
Scotland, U.K.

Typeset and printing by Meigle Printers, Tweedbank Industrial Estate, Galashiels, Scotland.

A SCOTTISH WEDDING

CONTENTS

ISBN: 0 9533975 0 5

INTRODUCTION

In the cycle of life between birth and death the single most important event to affect human beings is surely falling in love. It is not unnatural or unexpected that this joyfull experience be celebrated and rejoiced.
In Scotland as in other countries around the world the joining of man and woman has long been celebrated and proclaimed. Indeed the public proclamation of the contract has importance not only as a declaration of love and committment but also to make known to the society in which the man and woman live that their status has now changed; that they are no longer single and no longer available to be courted or to court.

A prime purpose of marriage is the begetting of children. The continuation of life is vital to the survival of not only the individual line but to the tribe or society. Fertility is thus central in marriage, in the rituals and celebrations of marriage and is a powerful motivation underlying the uniting of man and woman. Despite the censorious efforts of all kinds of moral and social *'improvers'* and producers of romantic fiction the honest enjoyment of human sexuality and fertility remains constant; as it always has been and always will be.

The conventional wedding of today is a curious mixture of romance, ritual, religion, superstition and practicality. Many of the rules of etiquette, practices and paraphenalia we take for granted without realising that they may have meaning and purpose deeply rooted in the past. By examining the ancient wedding customs of Scotland we can gain insight into the traditions which have come down to us and understand the meaning of the rituals and symbols.

1—COORTIN

At the risk of being obvious, before there can be a bridal there has to be a couple to be married and courting is the inevitable preamble to the married state. Sexuality and courtship have many pitfalls and it is not surprising to find an abundance of old Scots rhymes, sayings and songs warning or advising on the best ways of securing a mate or of the consequences of pre-marital sex. Magic and divination were used to foretell the future and all means were taken by young women to avoid bad luck and the risk of becoming an old maid. Some proverbial sayings are as follows:-

'Mim-moued maidens n'er get a man
Muckle moued maids get twa'

'She's ower mony werrocks to get a man' (werrock = wrinkle)

'Marry for love and work for siller'

'They say in Fife
That next tae nae wife
The best thing is a guid wife'

'When ye tak a man, ye tak a maister'

'Change the name and no the letter
Change for the waur and no the better.' 23

Means were frequently taken to find out who was to be the future husband or wife. There were various ways of doing this. Some of the incantations could be performed at any time whilst others could only be done on Halloween. Here are some that can be used at any time:-

'The first time a girl slept in a strange bed a ring was put on the finger, one of the shoes was placed below the bed, the bed was entered backwards. The future husband would then be seen in a dream.'

'The maid who was desirious of seeing who was to be her future husband had to read the third verse of the seventeenth chapter of the Book of Job after supper; wash the supper dishes and go to bed without the utterance of a single word, placing below her pillow the Bible, with a pin stuck

through the verse she had read. The future husband would appear in a dream.'

'The first time the note of the cuckoo was heard the hearer turned round three times on the left heel against the sun, searched in the hollow made by the heel and in it a hair of the colour of the future husband or wife was found.'

'To find out whether the lover would remain true and become the husband, three stalks of the Carl-doddie or Ribwort, were taken when in bloom. They were stripped of their blossom, laid in the left shoe which was placed under the pillow. If the lover was to become the husband, the three stalks were again in full bloom in the morning. If the lover was to prove untrue the stalks were without blossom.'

The following were only effective if performed on Halloween:-

'Pullin the Castoc' - with eyes blindfolded, the first stock of cabbage or greens touched in the kailyard was pulled. According to the quantity of earth and the shape of the stock (ill or well formed) augured the amount of worldly means and comliness of the future husband or wife. The stock was then placed inside the house door and the baptismal name of the young man or woman, who entered first after it was placed was to be the baptismal name of the husband or wife.'

'Sowing lint seed' - When evening was drawing to night the maiden had to steal out quietly with a handful of lintseed and walk across the ridges of a field sowing the seed and repeating the words -

"Lint seed I saw ye,
Lint seed I saw ye,
Lat him its to be my lad,
Come aifter me and pu me'

On looking over the left shoulder she saw the apparition of him who was to be her mate crossing the rigs, in the act of pulling flax.'

'Fathoming a Rick' - This incantation was performed by measuring or fathoming with the arms round a stack of oats or barley, three times, against the sun. In going round the third time the apparition of the future

husband or wife was clasped when the arms were stretched for the last time.'

'Winning the Blue-clue' - The person had to go to the kiln secretly and in the gloamin, carrying a clue of blue worsted thread. This clue was cast into the kiln-logie. The end was retained and the performer unrolled the clue, forming a new one. Towards the end it was held tight. It was then demanded who held the thread. A voice answered, giving the name of the future husband or wife.'

'Winnowing Corn'- Go to the barn secretly and open both doors as if preparing to winnow corn. Take a sieve and three times go through the motion of winnowing corn. The apparition of the future husband entered by the one door to the windward, passed through the barn and made his exit by the other door.'

'Washing the sleeve of the shirt' - The maiden went to a south running stream, or to a ford where the living and dead crossed and washed the sleeve of her shirt. She returned home put on a large fire and hung the shirt in front of it. She went to bed, and from it kept a careful watch. The apparition of him who was to be her future husband came and turned the wet sleeve.'

'Roasting Peas' - A live coal was taken and two peas were placed on it; the one to represent the lad and the other the lass. If the two rested on the coal and burned together the two represented would become man and wife; and from the length of time the peas burned and the brightness of the flame the length and happiness of the married life could be determined. If one of the peas started off from the other there would be no marriage.'

'Eating an apple in front of a looking glass'- This was done in secret.An apple was taken and sliced off in front of a looking glass. Each piece before being eaten was stuck on the point of a knife and held over the left shoulder while at the same time combing the hair. The spectre of the husband would appear behind, stretching forth his hands to lay hold of the piece of apple.'

'By Three Cups or Wooden Basins' - Three wooden basins were placed in a line on the hearth; one was filled with pure water another with dirty and the third left empty. The performer was blindfolded and a wand or stick put into her hand. She was led up to the cups where she pointed to

one of them. This was done three times, the position of the cups being changed each time. 'The best of three' decided her fate, i.e. choosing the same cup twice. The choice of the cup with pure water indicated an honourable marriage; the choice of that with the dirty water betockened marriage, but in dishonour. If the choice fell on the empty cup a single life was to be the lot.' 24

More sinister are the love potions, two of which are as follows

'The root of the orchid were dug up. The old root is exhausted and when cast in water floats - this is hatred. The new root is heavy and sinks in water -this is love because nothing sinks deeper than love. The 'Love Root' was dried ground and secretly administered as a potion; strong love was the result.'

'Two lozenges were taken, covered with perspiration (or other bodily juices)and stuck together and given in this form to the one whose love was sought. The eating of them excited strong affection.'

Unluckily for these two charms, marriage dissipates them turning love to hatred.
Other omens were observed such as these;-

'When a live coal tumbles from the fire onto the hearth towards one who is unmarried it is regarded as a token that marriage is at hand. Hence the saying 'Fire bodes marriage.'

'When a young womans apron string or garter unloosened itself, she was at that time the subject of her lovers thoughts.'

In an age of reason these beliefs seem superstitious and foolish, but we can be sure that great store was put on such means and methods. These things were very firmly believed in.The rituals and beliefs almost all contain some elements of the occult - the number three, anticlockwise motion (widdershins), running water, the left side (sinistra), fire and water - and have parallels in witchcraft rites and spells.
Survivals of these customs persist such as at Halloween parties and if we are to be honest superstition still plays a large part in our lives and as we shall see, particularly in the wedding ritual.
Pre-marital intercourse was as popular in the past as today but with different problems and consequences. Young lads would shout at courting couples the following lines;-

"Lad and lass
Wi the fite cockade
Mairrit in the coal hole
An kirkit in the barn'
or
"Cockie doss,Lad and Lass
Mairrit in a coal hole.' 25

Some old songs also give an insight into the ways of courting.

THERE CAM A YOUNG MAN

There cam a young man to my daddies door
My daddies door,my daddies door
There cam a young man to my daddies door
Came seeking me to woo

Chorus
And wow he was a braw young lad
A brisk young lad,and a braw young lad
And wow he was a braw young lad
Came seeking me to woo

But I was baking when he came
When he came, when he came
I took him in an gaed him a scone
To thaw his frozen mou

I set him in aside the bink
I gaed him bread and ale to drink
And ne'er a blyth styme wad he blink
Until his wame was fu

Gae get ye gone, ye cauldrife woo'er
Ye sour lookin, cauldrife woo'er
I straightway showed him to the door

There lay a duck-dub before the door
Before the door, before the door
There lay a duck dub before the door
And there fell he I trow

Out came the goodman and high he shouted
Out came the goodwife and low she louted
And a the town neighbours were gathered about it
And there lay he I trow

Ye came to woo but ye're a beguiled
Ye ave fa'en i the dirt and ye're a befyld
We'll hae nae mair of you. 26

The wooer is rejected and bettered but in the following song with its delicate understatement it is the maid who suffers.

There gaed a fair maiden out to walk
In a morning of July
She was fair, bonnie, sweet and young
But met wi a lad unruly

He took her by the lily white hand
He swore he looed her truly
The man forgot but the maid thought on
O it was in the month of July. 27

Longing for the loved one is beautifully expressed in the old song;

WAT AND WEARY

O wat wat - o wat and weary
Sleep I can get nane
For thinking on my dearie
A the night I wak

A the day I weary
Sleep I can get nane
For thinking on my dearie. 28

Willingness and practicality are expressed in the song;

I LOOED N'ER A LADDIE BUT ANE

I looed ner a laddie but ane
He loes ner a lassie but me
He is willing to make me his ain
And his ain I'm willing to be

He has coft me a rockly o blue
And a pair o mittens o green
The price was a kiss o my mou
And I paid the debt yestreen

My mithers aye making a fraise
Saying I'm oer young to be wed
But lang eer she counted my days
O me she was brought to bed

So had your tongue dear mither
And dinna be flyting sae bauld
For we can do the thing when we're young
That we canna do weel when we're auld. 29

Similar sentiments but put more succinctly are those from Robert Burns' mother;

Kissin is the key of love
And clappin is the lock
And makin O is the best thing
That ere a young thing got. 30

Tocher or Dowry

The offer of material wealth as an aid to courtship is found in several old songs such as;

I hae layen three herring a salt
Bonnie lass, gin yell take me tell me now
And I hae brownd three pickles o maut
And I cannae cum ilka day to woo. 31

JOCKEY SAID TO JENNY

Jocky said to Jenny, Jenny wilt thou do it?
Ne'er a fit quo Jenny, for a my tocher good
For a my tocher good, I winna marry thee
E'ens ye like quo Jocky, ye may let it be
I hae gowd and gear, I hae land enough
I hae seven good owsen ganging in a pleugh

Ganging in a pleugh and linking ower the lee
And gin ye winna tak me I can let ye be. 32

The Bannatyne manuscript of 1568 includes an old poem called 'the Wooing of Jenny and Jock' which also tells of this process of materialistic practicality in choosing a mate. 33

Pre-marital Sex

But some times the process of coortin goes badly wrong as told in the song

UP STAIRS , DOWNSTAIRS

As I came in by Fisherraw
Musselburgh was near me
I threw aff my mussel pock
And courted wi my dearie

O had her apron bidden down
The kirk wad neer hae kend it
But since the words gane thro the toun
My dear I canna mend it

But ye maun mount the cutty stool
And I maun mount the pillar
ŠAnd thats the way that poor folks do
Because they hae nae siller
Chorus
Up stairs down stairs
Timber stairs fears me
I thought it lang to ly my lane
When I'm sae near my dearie. 34

and in

JENNY NETTLES

Saw ye Jenny Nettles
Jenny Nettles, Jenny Nettles
Coming frae the market
Bag and baggage on her back

Her fee and bountith in her lap
Bag and baggage on her back
And a baby in her oxter

I met ayont the kairney
Jenny Nettles, Jenny Nettles
Singing till her bairnie
Robin Rattles bastard
To slee the dool upo the stool
And ilka ane that mocks her
She round about seeks Robin out
To stop it in his oxter

Fy, Fy! Robin Rattle
Robin Rattle, Robin Rattle
Fy, Fy! Robin Rattle
Use Jenny Nettles kindly
Score out the blame and shun the shame
An without mair debate o't
Tak hame your wain make Jenny fain
The leel and leesome gate o't. 35

Thus the courting and its various outcomes. We see in the song 'Jockey said to Jenny' the process of making pledges or surities in the form of goods or gear and the use of the *'Tocher'* or dowry as a bargaining device.

This began to be formalised with the exchange of love tokens as a promise of marriage or betrothal. The materialism of the deal being symbolised by the exchange of silver sometimes a divided sixpence or in the poorer class by the exchange of spoons. An old song tells us;-

"I sit at my creepie and spin at my wheel
And think on the laddie that looed me sae weel
He had but ae sixpence he brak it in twa
And he gied me the half o't when he gaed awa

LUCKENBOOTH BROOCHES

The idea of silver as a betrothal token was taken a step further in the late 17th Century by the introduction of Luckenbooth Brooches. These were small in size sometimes very small and were principally made of silver, frequently engraved and occasionally enriched with garnets crystals and coloured glass. They derived their name from the Luckenbooths, a narrow range of buildings close to St Giles Church in Edinburgh where many of the jewellers and silversmiths of the late seventeenth and eighteenth centuries had their booths. They were principally love tokens or betrothal brooches and the prevailing form was that of a heart or two hearts intertwined. This custom seems to have given way in the 19th Century to the giving of engagement rings as the once Royal style of giving *'ingagement'* rings filtered down the social scale.

Luckenbooth Brooch by The Moffatt Family, The Johnnie Armstrong Gallery, Henderson's Knowe, Teviothead, by Hawick, Roxburghshire, Scotland, TD9 0LF. tel 01450 850237. Designers in Gold and Silver, Celtic, Viking and Scottish jewellery.

2—PREPARATION

When the 'coortin' had been successfully completed the marriage was commonly arranged between the two parties without the knowledge of the parents. At times the mothers might be let into the secret, but it was only after the main arrangements had been made that the fathers were informed.

Choosing the Day

The marriage day was usually a weekday, rarely a Saturday and never on the Sabbath. The time chosen for the marriage was important. May was a month to be avoided as the proverb *'Marry in May and rue the day'* reminds us. It is probably true to this day that fewer marriages are made in May than in any other month of the year. This is not peculiar to Scotland but is a belief of old standing. In Rome it was a proverbial saying that only ill-omened women marry in May. *'Mense malas maio nubere vulgu ait'* appears in Ovid and was affixed to the gates of Holyrood Palace on the morning of 16th May the day after the marriage of Mary Queen of Scots and Bothwell. Other versions of the rhyme are *'Marry in May, You'll rue it for aye'* and *'Marry in May, The bairns will aye waste awa''*. This last warning is probably the real reason for the warning - a child conceived in May would be born in January -the harshest month of the year.

The period of the increasing moon was regarded as lucky. The people would have regarded it as tempting fate if they had embarked on matrimony at a time when the moon was on the wane. Every great enterprise was undertaken when that orb was growing. It was also unlucky for two of a family to be married during the same year.

The Banns

The date of the marriage being fixed, it was and still is necessary to put in the banns or *'the cries'*; the notification to the minister to proclaim the banns of marriage. This was variously called *'the Contrack night'* or *'the beuckin night'*. The bridegroom, if at all possible, presented himself at the home of the bride along with a few friends. Accompanied by the brides father or other relative, the young man went to the session clerk to

give in the name, for proclamation or as it was called *'to lay down the pawns'*. 38

An intended marriage would be announced informally by the local children singing the following;

Braw news is come to town
Braw news is carried
Braw news is come to town
Jennys to be married

First she got the kail pot
Syne she got the ladle
Syne she got a dainty wean
And syne she got a cradle. 39

The Feet Washing

Either on the Contrack night or on the night before the wedding at the bride or bridegrooms parents home a convivial group of friends and relatives would gather. The food was plain (perhaps dried fish and tatties) and there was much teasing and innocent merriment one outstanding and widespread part of the programme was *'the feet-washing'* of the bridegroom. This entailed removing the bridegrooms shoes and stockings and plunging his feet in water and smearing with soot or shoe blacking. It would seem that this performance varied in severity from plain soap to mixtures of black lead and treacle.The victim always struggled but despite his efforts the process was always very thoroughly carried out. 40

This seems to have been the survival of an ancient custom. The soot with which the limbs were smeared was believed to possess magical virtue as connected with the hearth and fire and may have been held to *'neutralise the mutual dangers of contact'*. To this day young men on their stag night are often given a similar treatment. 41

The Waddin Sark

In the North East of Scotland another custom was prevalent. This was the gift of the *'Waddin Sark'* by the bride to the bridegroom. He on his part provided her with a wedding dress. We may observe that the gift of the shirt was more than the evidence of the young womans skill in needlework. Its acceptance was a pledge of marriage and it was not unknown for a marriage to be broken off owing to a difference of opinion as to this ancient practice. 42

The Providan

In the interval between the final contract of marriage and its celebration the young woman was busy getting in order all her *'providan'* for her future home. One or more days were given to the *'thiggan'* of wool from her friends and neighbours. If she had been thrifty, her feather bed, bolster, pillows, blankets, sheets etc would have been ready in anticipation of the coming event.On a day some weeks before the marriage the bridegroom, accompanied by the brides mother and sisters went to a neighbouring village to buy *'the bonnie things'*, that is the bridal dress etc, when it was the custom for the young man to present dresses to the bride and bride's mother. Besides the *'providan'* the young woman bought a chest of drawers or a kist. All the providan was sent to the future home a few days before the marriage and it was sent unlocked and unbound. To have sent it locked or bound would have boded a marriage of difficulty and travail.

Invites

The guests were invited by the bride and bridegroom. The bride commonly alone but sometimes with her best maid called on her friends and gave them a personal invitation. She had in addition to chose two young men to lead her to church (the sens). The bridegroom likewise alone or with his best man gave personal invitations to his party and at the same time asked two young women to lead him to church. This *'biddin'* was always subject to good natured teasing. 43

The last person to be invited was said to have received the *'Pipers Bid'* or *'Pipers Invite'*. 44

It was also considered unlucky to invite the minister before all the other invitations and arrangements had been made. It was usual to have the minister of the bride conduct the service but there was one exception to this rule. If the minister was newly ordained to the charge, then amongst those who adhered to the old beliefs, only misfortune would follow if he were to officiate. 45

A very general invitation was given to weddings and often the whole community might have attended. It was customary for each guest to make a present, contribute to the payment of the piper or pay a lawin. The present usually took the form of something required for the marriage feast, such as a fowl, a few pounds of butter, cheese, whisky etc. The present was often reserved until the morning of the marriage day when there was a rivalry as to who should give hansel, i.e. be first to give the gift to the bride or bridegroom. Some bridals seem to have been run in business like manner and prices were charged and indeed fixed by the authorities, hence the name *'penny bridal'* or *'siller bridal'*. 46

Signs and Omens

Great preparations were made for the feast and from the brewing of the bride ale and the baking of the bridal bread omens were drawn. With respect to the ale, if the wort boiled up on the far side of the pot it was accounted unlucky, if in the front, lucky. If it fermented strongly or as it was expressed it was strong on the barm good fortune was augured. It was the same if the ale was strong when presented at the feast. In baking the cakes great care was taken with the first cake lest it should be broken - a broken cake portending unhappiness. 47

There were many other signs, omens and customs which had to be attended to before marriage.
On no account must the bride and groom meet on the marriage day till they meet on the bride-stool. Such a meeting would have been followed by some calamity or series of calamities. The state of the weather was watched closely. There might be heard expressions such as *'He's gloomin sair on her,'* if the day was dull , or *'He's blinkin fell cantie on her'*, if it were alternate bright and dull. *'She's greetin unco sair'*, if the day was rainy. A shower of rain was held to be lucky, however;

'Happy's the corpse, an happy's the bride,
That gets a shoor i' thir side'.

A bright sunny day indicated great happiness;

'Happy's the bride the sun shines on,
Happy's the corpse the rain falls on.' 48

The bride was usually dressed by her maids, and every article of dress must be new. The bridal dress could on no account be worn before it was required. When it came to be put on and if it did not fit it could not be cut or altered but only adjusted the best way possible. If the marriage shoes were too small, evils were boded.

Something borrowed must be worn; a ring was accounted of most virtue.
'Something old something new, something borrowed something blue'

Thus goes the well known rhyme - but why these charms? The following may offer some explanation.
Something old - we have noticed the ban on a new minister officiating but in old belief there seems to have been a widespread objection to newness e.g. *'It is said that the first child baptised in a new font is sure to die'*. There still is a widespread suspicion of newness and change. The old thus represents tradition, continuity and respect for the past.
Something new - this is the opposite power - the virginal, the future.
Something borrowed - This I think represents debt or a reminder that the bride owes something to the community and to her family. Something blue - this is from ancient colour symbolism.Certain colours were attributed specific powers and are given in the following rhyme;
'Blue
'S love true
Green
'S love deen
Yellow
'S forsaken'

Green also symbolised fertility and we shall see how it was used in other parts of the wedding celebration. It is worth noting that if a younger sister was to be married before an elder sister she had to give her sister green garters.

Once these many matters had been attended to the wedding could proceed.

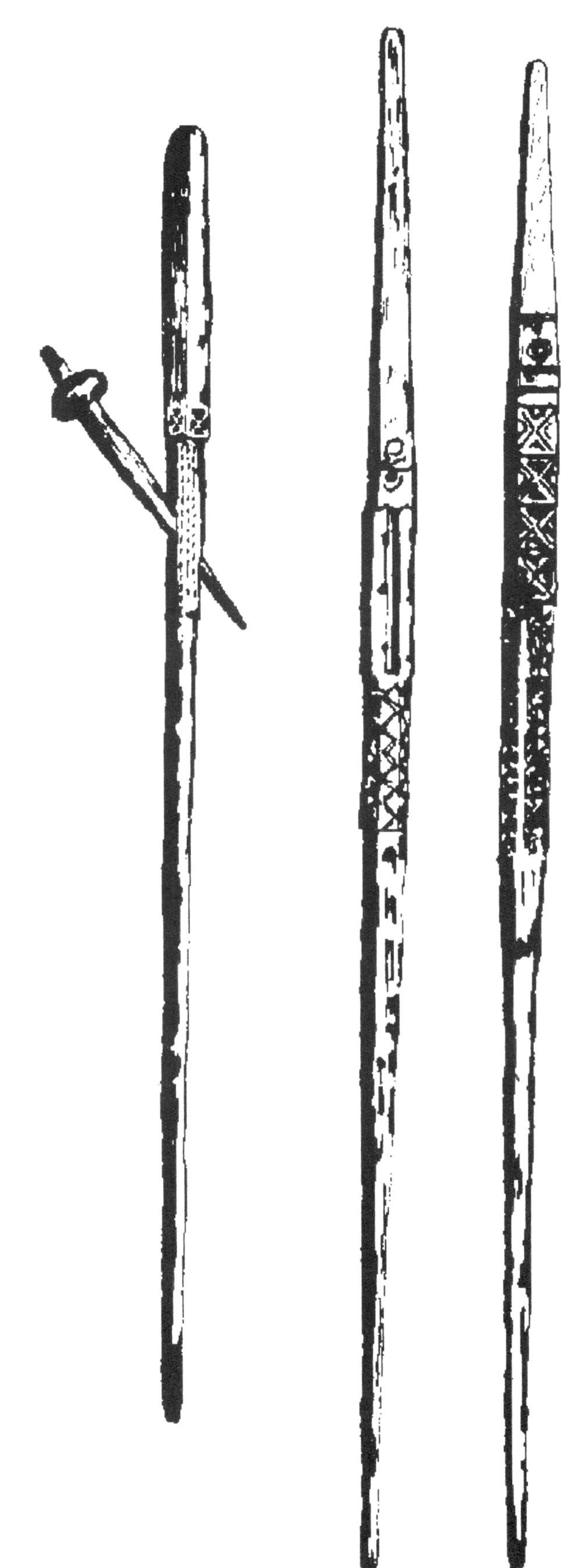

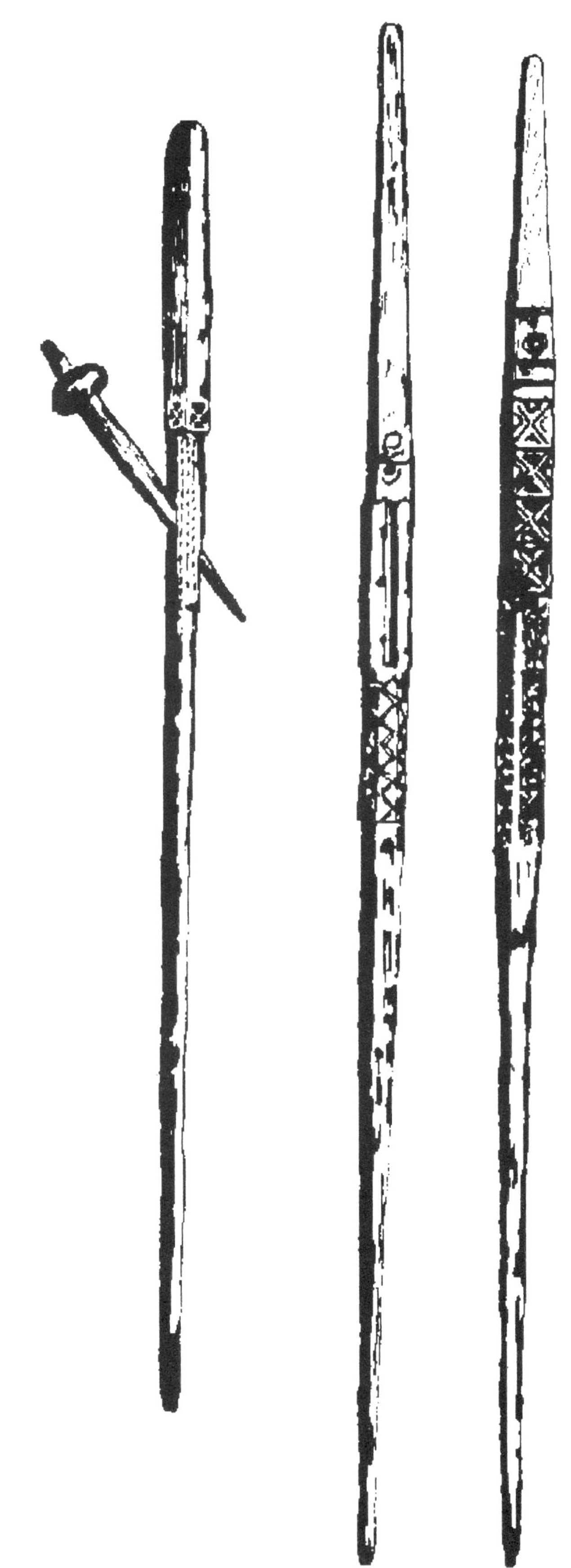

3—WEDDING CEREMONIAL

Old style marriage was a community affair. Sometimes the population of a fishing village, sometimes the inhabitants of a rural district. Marriage was a ceremonial with which all were concerned. The whole tribe was involved. The wedding was a day of public celebration.
It would appear that in the customs of the Germanic peoples (Anglo-Saxon) who came to be the dominant cultural group in Lowland Scotland, marriage had three separate components.
The first of these was the *'bewedding'* where *'weds'* (Old English 'weddian' = to pledge, Germanic, 'wadhjam' = a pledge) or surety was given by the bridegroom to the bride's father in the form of pledges or gifts. To recognise that this had taken place to everyone's agreement pierced stones (rings) were exchanged. 7

The second component was the giving away of the bride to the bridegroom by the bride's father. This was conducted as a separate ceremony and was concluded by *'hand-faestung'* - the joining of hands to seal the contract.

The third part of the marriage was the bridal (Old English *'bryd ealu'* = brides ale drinking).

There is a common misconception that handfasting was a trial marriage this was not the case. Until 1940 in Scottish Civil Law contract by consent constituted a valid marriage as did marriage by habit and repute. There were however early enactments which tried to force handfast marriages to be regularised in Church such as this enactment at Aberdeen in 1562;

Item - Because syndrie and many within this toun are handfast, as thai call it, and made promis of marriage a long space bygone, som sevin yeir, sum six yeir, sum longer, sum schorter, and as yit will nocht marry and compleit that honorable bond, neither for fear of God nor luff of that party, but lyis and continewis in manifest fornication and huirdom; heirfor it is statut and ordanit, that all sic personis as hes promesit marriage faithfully to compleit the same betwix this and Fasterns Eve nixt. (They also forbade people who had exchanged promises of marriage to have intercourse together). 9

Despite the efforts of the Church the old rules remained part of the secular law of Scotland until as recently as 1st July 1940. There is also evidence to show that the Reformed Church compromised in their form of marriage to accomodate common law and practice.
In the Form of Marriage used by the reformed Church there was no declaration on the part of the Minister that the parties were now man and wife. In Scotland the declaration would have been superfluous as it would be commonly recognised that *'consent makes marriage'*, and that once consent had been publicly announced the marriage was complete. This was quite in accordance with the law and practice of the Medieval Church and remains the basis of the law of marriage in Scotland. It should also be observed that the taking by the hand is still in use among all denominations in Scotland. The giving away of the bride by her father or nearest male relative has also persisted. The civil use and exchange of rings also remains a significant feature of marriage.
The old wedding customs survived longest in rural areas and in the early years of this century writers could quote the memories of old people such as Dr Rories old lady informant aged 75 living in Auchterderran in Fife. 23
In the North East of Scotland up until the end of the 19th Century the following custom prevailed. The day would begin by the arrival of the guests at an early hour, those invited by the bride at her home and those invited by the bridegroom at his. Breakfast would be served consisting of oatmeal porridge. After breakfast it was not unusual for all to join in dancing till the hour of going to church came. At the appointed time, if the marriage was to be in the Kirk, two men called *'sens'* were dispatched from the house of the bridegroom to demand the bride. On making their appearance a volley of fire-arms met them. When they came up to the door of the brides' home they asked;
"Does (Jenny) bide here?'
"Aye,what dae ye want wi her?'
"We want her for (Jock)',
"Bit ye winna get her',
"But we'll tak her'.
"Will ye come in,an taste a moothfu o' a dram till we see aboot it?'

And so the sens entered the house and got possession of the bride. 50

In the Biggar area up until at least the mid 19th Century if the wedding was to be at the brides house the bridal party assembled at the house of the bridegroom, and preceded by a young man with a white rod called

'the saine' or *'sign'* and headed by a piper or fiddler, set out in order of procession to the house of the bride.
The references to *'Sens', 'Saines' or 'Signs'* would appear to be derived from the ancient Celtic priests called in Gaelic *'Sennachie'* or guide who as a symbol of their office carried a white rod.
Both parties if going to church, arranged their departure from their respective homes in such a way as to arrive at church about the same time. The brides party always having the preference. The bride supported by the sens walked at the head of her party and when she set out she was on no account to look back. The bridegroom supported by two young maidens walked at the head of his party. On leaving a few old besoms or scrubbers were thrown after both bride and groom. 52
(This symbolised the surrender of the legal right of the parents over their children.)
In Fife the bride and groom were sometimes *'bowered'* i.e. having an arch of green boughs held over their heads and all the couples went *'traivlin linkit'* (walking arm in arm). 53
A member of both the brides party and the grooms carried a bottle of whisky and a glass and another carried bread and cheese. The first person met was treated. Great attention was paid to the *'First Fit'*. A man on horseback was deemed most lucky. Each party was accompanied by pipers and a constant firing of guns was kept up. Every means was employed to keep off evil spirits.

The Church authorities disliked these practices; In 1645 the Kirk Session of Queensferry in West Lothian ordained that;
'parties who are to be married shall have no pipers to convey them to the Kirk, nor play at all to them in the street, nor at dinner or supper or anywhere else...' 54a

At Banchory - Devenick in 1732 two men were found guilty of firing pistols in time of worship at a marriage in church. In 1839 the same Session forbade all shooting at marriages. 54

In the Parish of Auchterdennan in Fife it was the rule that all shooting (owing to damage having on one occasion been done to the sacred edifice) cease when the procession came in sight of the Kirk. 55

The custom continued in many parts of the country long after the reason for its observance was forgotten and elements of these customs persist today in the tying of cans and shoes to the wedding car.

The Kirk being reached, the beadle or bellman would be in attendance to lead the bridegroom to the *'Bride-steel'* or bride-stool, that is the pew that was set aside for the use of those who were to be married. The bride was then led forth and placed next to the bridegroom. Great care was used to have her placed a the proper side to have done otherwise would have been a very bad omen. Next to the bride stood her *'best maid'*. This office, though accounted an honour, was not without risk. If the bride was expectant the maid would within a year fall into the same disgrace. Three times a bridesmaid was the inevitable prelude to remaining unmarried. Next to the bridegroom stood the *'Best young man'*. 56

The Reformation took place in Scotland in 1560 but its effect was not immediate or all embracing. It took time for power and influence of the reformers to take hold and for their ideology to be accepted.

The form of marriage used by the Reformed Church is contained in the Book of Common Order and is identical with that in the Book of Geneva, based on liturgy by Calvin and Farel in 1533.As early as 1571 the General Assembly ordained that all marriages were ; *'to be solemnised according to the order published'* and that *'all marriages be solemnised in face of congregation'* stating in doing so that troubles and slander had risen because Ministers had married couples in private houses. It is clear that Presbyterian Divines held to a very high view of marriage. In all their doings there was an obsessive rejection of *'papistical rites or superstitious acts'* of the Medieval Catholic Church. 6

These superstitious and papistical rites embraced not only the customs and practice of the Medieval Christian Church but also the age old Anglo Saxon and Celtic customs such as handfasting. Like the Medieval Church the Reformers insisted that marriage must be made in Church and any attempt to perform the service elsewhere met with their strong disapproval. Their wish was to regularise marriage and to have it recognised and recorded in the sight of God and Congregation.

After 1560 the Form of Marriage in the Book of Common Order of the Reformed Church of Scotland required that marriage would take place *'at the beginning of Sermon'*. The service proper would begin with an exhortation taken in part from the Anglican Prayer Book. Thereafter the Minister, speaking to the parties about to be married, required them to state whether they know any impediment why they should not be joined together.(This charge is taken word for word from the English Book). A similar question was then put to the congregation and if no impediment was alleged the Minister required the man to state whether he takes the

woman for his wife, the answer being, *'Even so I take her before God and in the presence of this his Congregation'.* After a similar question had been put to and a similar reply received from the woman, there was read over our Lord's words regarding marriage from the 19th Chapter of the Gospel according to St Matthew, the reading being prefaced thus;

'Give diligent ear then to the Gospel that ye may understand how our Lord would have this Holy contract kept and observed and how sure and fast a knot it is which in no wise be loosed. Our Lord sayeth; that he which made them at the beginning made them male and female, and said, for this cause shall a man leave mother and father and shall cleave to his wife: and they twain shall be one flesh. Wherefore they are no more twain but one flesh, what therefore God hath joined together let not man put assunder'.(Matthew 19)

This portion read, the minister proceeds;
'If ye assuredly believe these words..then may ye be certain that God hath even so knit you together in this Holy estate of wedlock; wherefore apply yourselves to live together in Godly love, in Christain peace, and good example...even as Gods'word doth appoint'.
"The Lord sanctify and bless you, the Lord pour the riches of his Grace upon you, that ye may please him and live together in Holy love to your lives end. So be it.' 57

The 128th Psalm would then be sung.

'Bless'd are they that fears the Lord
And walketh in his ways
For of thy labour thou shalt eat
And happy be always.
Thy wife shall be a fruitful vine
By thy house sides be found
Thy children like to olive plants
About thy table round.' 58

At the beginning of Sermon and doubtless in the ordinary devotions Prayers suitable to the occasion would be offered. If more than one couple were married in Church at the same time, there were often unseemly scenes before the close of the marriage service. Some of the parties would be making for the door before the benediction was pronounced, the reason being, that in popular belief, the first out of church carried off the blessing.

At Elgin on 13th July 1632, William Adam is fined by the Session for his *'uncomely behaviour in the Kirk after a marriage in pressing to be the first to be at the door'.*
This was so frequent an offence there, that in 1638 on the occasion of three marriages, the contracting parties were *'acted not to make tumult nor strive for place at going out at the Kirk doors under pain of 40s each man for himself.'* 59

Once outside the Kirk the minister frequently kissed the bride and in certain districts the bride pinned a marriage favour to the ministers right arm. The two would receive the congratulations of all present. The bridegroom would pay the beadle his fee and dispense the *'ba-siller'*. The local children would assemble round the door and demand *'ba-siller'*; a handful of coins would be thrown and a mellee would ensue. This practice still continues in the rural areas but has disappeared in the cities due to the dangers of motor cars becoming too great. 60

The procession would then reform, led by the bride supported by the sens. Then followed the bridegroom, supported by the brides' two best maidens; and with music and the firing of guns and pistols the two parties, now united, marched along the main road to the home of the bridegroom. On no account was it allowed to take any by roads either going or coming from church and in some areas it was considered necessary for the party to cross running water twice in their journey. Some of the old tunes played by the piper for the wedding procession would certainly have included; *'Woo'ed an married an a', 'I hae a wife o my ain', 'The Rock and the Wee Pickle Tow' and 'Hey Ca thru'.*
Where appropriate the company would join in the words and chorus of these tunes.

As before, bread and cheese and a dram were given to the first fit on the homeward journey. On coming near the house the most athletic and courageous of the unmarried set off to *'run the brooze'* or *'win the kail'*. The runner who first reached the house of the bridegroom was the winner, and would be the first to be married. There is a parallel here with the first out of church custom . 61

When the bride arrived at her new abode she would be welcomed by the bridegroom's mother. On the passing of the bride over the threshold a piece of *'bride-cake'* would be broken over her head, emblematic of the plenty which it was hoped would always prevail in her dwelling. In some places bread and cheese were used and these were either held in a sieve above her or scattered around her. The pieces would be prized by the

young unmarried, who would place the piece beneath their pillows to *'dream on'*. This is the forerunner of the *'brides cake or wedding cake'*. 62
In the Lothians after the breaking of the *'infar-cake'* this rhyme was sung.

'Welcome to your ain fireside
Health and wealth attend the bride
Wanters noo your true wierd make
Joes are spaed by the infar-cake' 62a

This *'infar-cake'* or *'dreaming bread'* as it was called in Shetland was known in Roman times as confarreatio - marriage by offering of bread. The term *'confetti'* comes from this word. The modern paper confetti being the representation of the bread. 63
Crossing the threshold of the new home involved peril from unseen influences. The door of a house was always a danger point (witness the biblical mottos on door lintels in 17th and 18th Century Scots houses).To ensure the safety of the bride, she was carried over the threshold. Another preservative was a live coal or peat on the doorstep and often a cockerel was introduced to the house and would have to be ejected by the bride - a scape sacrifice, the bearer of all ill. 64
In some districts a Rock (distaff) charged with flax was borne before the bride as she came to her new home - a symbol that she was to be mindful of life by her labour. Thus the careful spinster became a thrifty housewife. To her new home she brought the emblems of Work, Worth and Warmth. The distaff would be placed above the door - a barrier to evil entering. 65

Having entered the new home, the bride was led to the hearth and the tongs put in her hands. With it she stirred the fire and again built it up. (The besom was sometimes substituted for the tongs, when she swept the hearth three times over.The crook or lum-click was then swung three times round her head, in the name of Father, Son and Holy Ghost and with the prayer *'May the Almighty mack this woman a guid wife'*.

Another method of *'saining'* the bride was observed in Buckie. A torch made of a fir stick; from which a knot had been ejected, leaving a hole, was lit by the mother in law of the bride. She whirled the lighted torch round the head of the young wife saying, *'I'm sayin'(saining) ye in the name of the Father, Son and Holy Ghost.'* 65a
This was practised about the mid 18th Century. The purpose of this fire purification was designed to make the new wife fruitful, through the

fertilising virtue of the fire. This would be in keeping with the purpose of other fire ceremonials.

The last act of the new wife's installation consisted of leading her to the *'girnal'* or *'mehl-bowie'* (meal bin) and pressing her hand into the meal as far as possible. This last action it was believed, secured in all time coming abundance of the staff of life in the household.
'Sain' is an old Anglo Saxon word which means to protect by divine power or enchantment. 66
With the new wife installed by the matriarch the scene would now be set for the Bridal.

THE BLYTHSOME BRIDAL

Fy let us a' to the bridal
For there will be lilting there
For Jocky's to be married to Maggie
The lass wi' the gowden hair
And there will be lang-kail and potage
And bannocks o' barley meal
And there will be good sawt herring
To relish a cog o' good ale

And there will be Saney the souter
And Will wi' the muckle mou
And there will be Tam the blutter
And Andrew the tinkler I trow;
And there will be bow'd legged Robbie
With thumbless Katies goodman
And there will be blue cheeked Dowbie
And Lawrie the Laird O' the land.

And there will be sow-libber Patie
And plooky-fac'd Wat i' the mill
Capper-nos'd Fracie and Gibbie
That wins in the howe of the hill;
And there will be Alaster Sibbie
Wha in with Black Bessie did mool
With snivelling Lilly and Tibby
The lass that stands aft on the stool.

And Madge that was buckled to Steenie
And coft him grey breeks to his arse

Wha after was hangit for stealing
Great mercy it happened nae worse;
And there will be gleed Geordy Janners
And Kirsh wi the lilly white leg
Wha gaed to the south for manners
And banged up her wame in mons-meg.

And there will be Juden McLawrie
And blinkin daft Barbara Mcleg
Wi flae lugged sharny faced Lawrie
An shangy mou'd Halucket Meg
And there will be happer ars'd Nansy
And fairy fac'd Flowrie by name
Muck Madie, and fat hippit Grisy
The lass wi the gowden wame/

And there will be girn again Gibbie
Wi his glaikit wife Jenny Bell
And misle-shin'd Mungo McApie
The lad that was skipper himsel
There lads and lasses in pearlings
Will feast in the heat o' the ha'
On sybows, and rifarts, and carlings
That are baith sodden and raw.

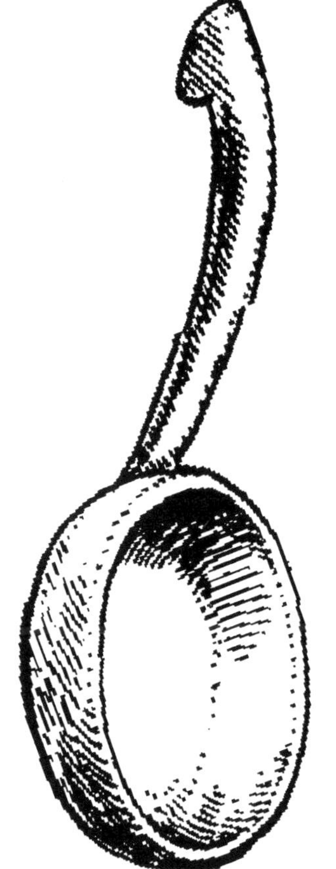

And there will be fadges and brachen
With fouth of good gabbocks and skate
Powfowdy, and drammock and crowdy
And caller nowt feet in a plate
And there will be partans and buckies
And whytens and speldings enew
With singed sheep-head and a haggies
And scadlips to suck till ye spew.

And there will be lapper'd milk kebbucks
And sowens and farles and baps
With swats and well scraped paunches
And brandy in stoups and in caps;
And there will be meal kail and castocks
With skink to sup till ye rive
And roasts to roast on a brander
Of fowks that were taken alive.

Scrapt haddocks, wilks, dulse and tangle
And a' mill o' good snishing to prie
When weary with eating and drinking
We'll rise up and dance till we die.
Then fy let us a' to the bridal
For there will be liltin there
For Jockys to be married to Maggie
The lass wi the gowden hair. [67]

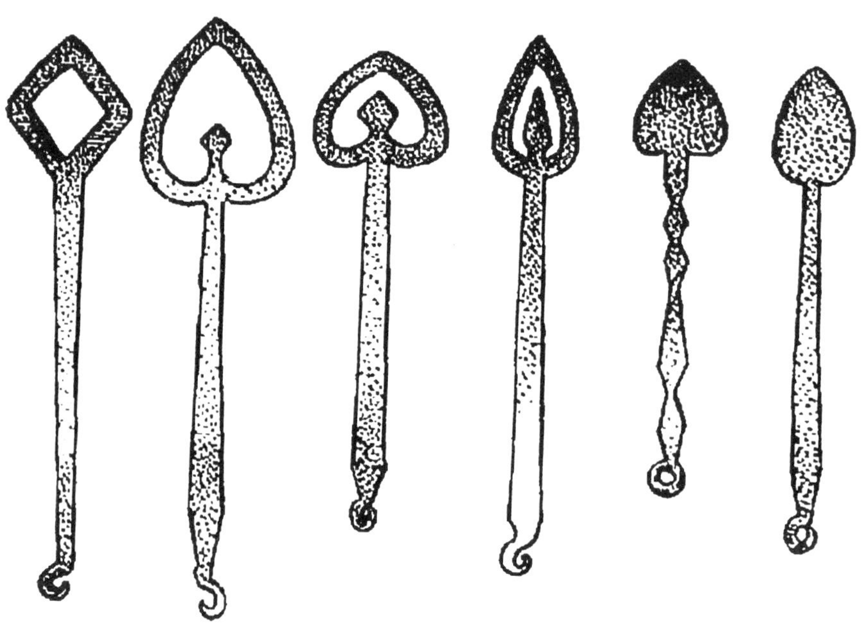

4—THE BRIDAL or THE PENNY WEDDING

'Fye let us a' tae the bridal'

'Ah she wad mak a' guid pipers bitch
For sniffin oot thae waddins.' (old proverb)

In Lowland Scotland the celebration of the union of man and woman has always been attended by a *'bridal'*. This is an old Anglo Saxon word and consists of two words co-joined; BRYD meaning bride or woman and EALO meaning ale or beer. Thus a bridal is a brides drinking party. Two things must be made clear; firstly it is the bride's celebration, she is the centrepiece - the queen. The bridegroom (bryd-gumma = brides man) is subservient for this day. Secondly it is a drinking party, not however a debauch. In pre-industrial society ale had a symbolic ritual significance. Ale or beer is made from bear meal or barley meal. A grain crop is the sustenance of life-the staff of life to all societies. Ale the ferment of that grain is the blood of life, the spirit of fertility. The bridal is therefore much more than its external trappings, it has deep psycho-social roots, entailing worship of the mysteries of life and the universe. When we drink to the health of the bride we salute not only womanhood and motherhood but also the Earth Mother.

In the past Lowland Scots weddings were called *'Penny Bridals'* or *'Siller Bridals'*. There is a great deal of information on them gathered by folklore researchers in the 18th and 19th Centuries and found in the records of the Kirk Sessions of the Reformed Church from 1580 onwards as they endeavoured to control such festivities.

It is difficult to say when Penny Bridals began or if weddings were ever otherwise. They were certainly the most important occasions for singing, dancing and festivities and were immensely popular. They were attended by whole communities, as many as two hundred participants being not uncommon. It seems that invitations, although given were not specifically required and everyone attending was expected to contribute, hence the name *'Penny Bridal'* or *'Siller Bridal'*.
The wedding celebration had economic motives. The greater the number attending the greater the sum collected for the married couple. The

monetary contribution was known in the Lowlands as the *'lawing'*. For example this extract from the records of Stirling-

'The magistates...considering the great abuses committed at penny weddings by extorting exhorbitant pryces for their lawings ordaines that noe person exact nor receive nae lawing nor price exceeding 8/- Scots frae each persone.'

It is enactments such as these by Civil and Church Authorities which tell us so much about the manners and customs of the bridals.An extract from the Regality Court Book of Kinneill in February 1670 provides a detailed account of the wedding feast.

'Anent the huge and exhorbitant pryces of penny brydells, made and sett within the foresaid bounds...hereby statuts, enacts and ordains that no persone or persones..exact or receave any more from ilk persone who comes to the said penny brydell for the brydell denner than the pryces respective underwritten, to wit.- ten shillings Scots money at the brydells within the said burgh of regality, and nyne shilling money foresaid at the brydells within the said baroni and those persones who maks and affords the said penny brydells are to furnish to each mease (table) consisting of four persons for the foresaid raites and pryces the particular victuals following - to wit; two plaitts full, of broath, ane soddin of beife, ane roast of mutton or veill, according to the season of the year; four wheat loaffes and ane quart of ale with sufficient trunchers, servitors and spoones: provyding nevertheless in caise the setters and makers of the said penny brydells provyd and affoord to ilk mease ane sufficient henn by and attour the victuals above specifeit then it shall be leisum for them to exact two shillings more.'

The bridal would be held in a barn when the marriage was at a farm. In villages the guests were at times divided into parties and the feast spread over several houses. Sometimes a *'change house'* or inn would be used and if the weather were amenable the event would be held on *'the green'*. Such feasts gave rise at times to a good deal of excess and as mentioned the Authorities enacted law after law to suppress them. Musicians and beggars were particularly singled out as trouble makers. At Cullen;

'the Session considering that many abuses are committed at penny weddings by a confluence of idle people that gather themselves mainly to hear the musick did and do hereby enact that whoever afterwards shall have pypers at their wedding shall forfeit their pauns.' 68

The custom at a bridal was to treat everyone as equal and no-one was turned away. Beggars commonly gathered together and were regaled most plentifully , punch or whisky not being spared on them. This gave rise to opportunism as expressed in the old song;

A BEGGING WE WILL GO

O' a' the trades that I do ken
The begging is the best,
For when the beggars weary
He can sit down and rest

Chorus;

To the begging we will go, will go
To the begging we will go,

If there's a waddin in a toun
I'll airt me to be there;
And pour my kindest benisons
Upon the winsome pair.

And some will gie me beef and bread
And some will gie me cheese
Syne I'll slip out amang the folk
And gather the bawbees.

And I will wallop out a dance
Or tell a merry tale
Till some gude fellow in my dish
Will pour a soup of ale. 69

At the feast the bride was placed at the seat of honour, the head of the table. The guests arranged themseves according to their fancy. The bridegroom did not take his seat at table. His charge was to serve and look after the comfort of the guests. 70

Food

By the standards of the time the feast was abundant. The first course would be milk broth made of barley; the second, barley broth made from beef mutton or fowls; the third course consisted of rounds of beef, legs of mutton and fowls by the dozen served with loaves and oatcakes. Last came the puddings swimming in cream. Home brewed ale flowed in abundance from first to last. When the tables were cleared big bottles of whisky were brought in and punch made up from them in wooden punch bowls. The cups were filled and handed round and the toasting commenced. First the health of the bride and groom was proposed. The cups were drunk off at once and the toast received with *'a' the honours three'*. Round after round was drunk, each to a toast or sentiment. This would be the time to begin the singing. Songs humourous, bawdy, cautionary and moral. 71

Songs

Perhaps the bridegroom or a relative might sing the old song well known in the mid 18th Century -

I HAE A WIFE O' MY AIN

I hae a wife o my ain
I'll be haddin tae naebody
I'll hae a pat and a pan
I'll borrow frae naebody. 73

Another song might follow-

SOME SAY THAT KISSINGS A SIN

Some say that kissings a sin
But I say that winna stand
It is a most innocent thing
And allowed by the laws of the land

If it were a transgression
The ministers it would reprove

But they their elders and session
Can do it as weel as the lave.

Its lang since it came into fashion
I'm sure it will never be done
As long as there's in the nation
A lad, a lass, wife or a loun.

What can I say more to commend it
Tho' I should speak all my life
Yet this will I say in the end o't
Let everyman kiss his ain wife. 74

Finally the bride might be persuaded to sing-

I GOTTEN THE LADDIE THAT I LIKED SAIR

I gotten the laddie that I liked sair
I gotten the laddie that I liked sair
I gotten the laddie that I liked sair
And I'll ne'er lie wi my auld minnie nae mair

The har'est it is shorn, the rigs they are bare
The har'est it is shorn, the rigs they are bare
The har'est it is shorn, the rigs they are bare
And I'll ne'er lie wi' my auld minny nae mair. 72

As the whisky flowed so would the songs. An older woman would doubtless sing the cautionary *'Rock and Wee Pickle Tow'*, a warning that womans work is never done. The hazards of sexual intercourse would be aired in *'I rede ye beware o' the ripples young man'*. (The ripples are the backache from too much sexual activity). The gamut of sexuality would be explored in humourous earthiness in *'Tail Toddle'*, *'Stumpie'*, *'Brose and Butter'*, *'The Ploughman'* and *'O wat ye what my minnie did'*. Other cautionary and humourous songs would follow - *'My wife's a wanton wee thing'*, *'O that I had ne'er been married'*, *'Woo'ed an married an a'*, ending up perhaps with a rendition of *'The malts aboon the meal the night'*.

Dancing

By then the floor would have been cleared to make way for the dancing. This dancing always began with the *'shaimit-reel'* or *'Brides Reel'* . This dance was performed by the bride, the bride's maidens, the bridegroom and the best young men. The music to which it was danced was called the *'shaim-spring'* and the bride had the priviledge of choosing the music. The male dancers then paid the musician his fee. In some districts the *'shaimit-reel'* was danced by the bride and her best maid with the two sens as partners. Perhaps harking back to some earlier Celtic custom.

In the Borders the first dance after the supper was *'The Bonny Breist Knots'* which was commenced by the Bride and Groom. In the West Highlands the dance was called *'The Wedding Reel'* and was danced as a reel of four by the bride, groom, bestman and maid.

After this dance was over the bride fixed a favour on the right arm of her partner in the dance and the best maid fixed one on the left arm of her partner. The two sens then paid the musician.

All the traditional reels and country dances would be performed at these country weddings, the foursome and eightsome reels and country dances such as Petronella, Strip the Willow, Triumph etc.

Frequently the bride and her maid asked if there were other young men who wished to earn favours. Two would jump to the floor dance with the bride and maid and earn the favours on the left arm. 75

For more on Traditional Scottish Dancing see Traditional Dancing in Scotland by J.P.Flett and T.M.Flett, London 1964.

Favours seem to have been of particular significance. In Fife even in 1903 *'the green garters'* (which had been knitted in anticipation by the best maid) were seruptitiously pinned onto the clothing of the elder unmarried sister or brother of the bride.When discovered they were removed and tied around the left arm and worn for the rest of the evening. 76

Green, of course, is the colour of fertility and growth and we might read into this custom the *'contagion'* of marriage. Indeed it was common for the unmarried women present to rub against the bride *'for luck'* as that would ensure their own early marriage. 77

Dancing would then carry on far into the morning with the utmost vigour. This would be where the pipers of fiddlers would earn their fee.

Pipers

Pipers were highly thought of and in great demand. The poetry of the 17th and 18th centuries gives a clear picture of the role of the piper at weddings.

'At brydells, when his face we saw,
Lads, lasses, bridegroom, bride and a',
Smiling, cry'd, Johnie come awa',
A welcome guest
The enchanting chanter out he'd draw
His pleased us best. 78

"An than besides his valiant acts,
At bridals he wan many placks,
He bobbed ay behind folks backs,
An shook his head.
Now we want many merry cracks
Fen Habbies dead.

He was conveyor of the bride,
With kittock hinging at his side.
About the Kirk he thought a pride
The Ring to lead.
But now we may gae but a guide
Fen Habbies dead. 79

'Now when their dinner they had done
Then Jock himself began t' advance
He bad the piper play up soon
For, be his troth, he wou'd gae dance
The piper piped till's wyme gripped
And a' the rout began to revel
The bride about the ring she skipped
Till out starts baith carle and cavel.' 80

'Sae Tam the piper did play
And ilka ane danc'd that was willing
And a' the lave ranked through
And they held the stoupy ay filling
The auld wives sat and they chew'd
And when the carles grew nappy
They danc'd as weel as they dow'd
Wi' a crack o' their thumbs and a kappie
The lad that wore the white band
I think they cau'd him Jamie Mather
And he took the bride by the hand
And cry'd to play up "Maggie Lauder'.' 81

In the Epitaph on Habbie Simpson the piper leads the bride around the Church. This has its parallel in other usage such as circling wells three times, and the superstition that it is unlucky to walk widdershins (anti-sunwise) around a church.
The other meaning of the Ring is perhaps the Brides Reel or the *'Shaimit-reel'* and it is most likely that this would have been originally a ring dance or carol (ca-reel?) going round sunwise and essentially a fertility rite.

The last person to be invited to a wedding was said to have received "the Pipers Invite'. It is apparent that it was customary to invite the piper last. It would be easy to jump to the conclusion that this was an insult and the piper was of little significance. However we know that the presence of a piper was essential if the event was to be celebrated properly and pipers were highly regarded. We must take it that being invited last bestowed a special honour and this is borne out when we find that it was also customary to ask the minister to officiate once all the guests had been invited.

The words minister and minstrel are synonymous. A minstrel was a minister of music and the use of the term underlines the fact that in the past music was more often than not the perogative of the priesthood. Music has power over people and has always been imbued with magic power. The practice of inviting the Christian minister last, overlays the previous Celtic custom of inviting the musician/priest last. As the minister was necessary to make the wedding complete so also was the minstrel. They were last to be asked because they would not refuse; to officiate was their duty.

There is so much evidence to suggest that music like almost every other aspect of life in pre-industrial society was imbued with magical powers. The ritual use of music, song and dance is common to all societies and so it was in Scotland. The wedding tunes invoked fertility and good fortune and must have been regarded as vital to the celebrations. It has been noted that the giving of favours by the bride imbued fertility and it will come as no surprise to learn that it was the custom to tie a piece of the brides garter around the pipes to impart *'fertility'* to the music.

'The piper at a wedding in Scotland has always a piece of the brides garter tyed about his pipes for good luck.' 83

The overt role of pipers as masters of the revel or ministers of music, explains why they were singled out for punishment and repression by the Chuch Authorities who must have seen them as subversives usurping the new order in which the minister of the church was the centrepiece. Not surprisingly then to find that revealed at 17th Century Witch Trials is the knowledge that the Devil plays the bagpipes or that the Devil's chief warlock is a pyper. In the concepts of the times when everything had an opposite; Good and Bad, Fire and Water, God and the Devil, the role transference of the piper from the white side of magic to the black was a useful ploy in the suppression of the older Celtic beliefs.

BRIDAL DANCES

Dancing has always been a major part of any wedding and in the past there were special dances of unique character performed at Bridals.

CUTTYMUN

One of these old dances was called *'Cutty Hunker'* or *'Cuttymun'*. In Alan Ramsay's 'Christs Kirk on the Green' 1716 it is mentioned in two verses;

'He fits the floor syne wi' the bride,
To Cuttymun and Treeladle,
Thick, thick that day.'
and
In the last verse of the old bawdy song 'Andro and his Cuttygun' we read-

'O some delights in Cuttie Stoup
And some delights in cuttie mun
But my delights in arselins coup
Wi' Andrew an' his cuttie gun.' 87

An old bagpipe reel survives called *'Cuttymun and Treeladle'*. The title is mnemonic to the tune suggesting an old song to the melody. *'Cuttymun and Treeladle'* is also stylistically very similar to another old reel *'Tail Toddle'* suggesting a common origin.

We are told that a curious dance was performed to the tune and was called Cutty Hunker Dance. It was performed by two dancers who would crouch down to an almost sitting posture, leaning the body forward and grasping their knees tight with both arms and then leaping from side to side all around the room in the most grotesque fashion imaginable. 85

It all seems curious and grotesque until one recalls that the crouched position was the normal position for giving birth in past time.The dance may therefore be seen as a fertility rite. (Dr Rorie in "The Mining Folk of Fife', tells us that; *'it was not uncommon for some women to desire to be confined kneeling in front of a chair, on the ground that 'a their bairns had come hame that way'. This position must have been very common at one time'.* 86

The title of the old tune *'Cuttymun and Treeladle'* means a short spoon and a wooden ladle. These were the principal implements used for eating and serving food in pre-industrial households. Men often carried their cutty spoons with them. There is symbolism involved in the title for in the past it was the custom for couples to exchange betrothal gifts. Invariably these would be spoons, sometimes elaborately carved and

often decorated with hearts and initials. Cuttymun, the horn spoon - given
by the female to the male and Treeladle, the wooden ladle - given by the male to the female.

THE BLYTHSOME BRIDAL

This type of symbolic or allegorical dance was not uncommon and often at bridals a dramatic interlude would be performed.Robert Burns witnessed one of these in Galloway;-
'A young fellow is dressed up like an old beggar; a peruke, commonly made of carded tow, represents hoary locks; an old bonnet; a ragged plaid or sourtout, bound with a straw rope for a girdle; a pair of old shoes, with straw ropes twisted around his ankles, as is done by shepherds in snowy weather; his face they disguise as like wretched old age as they can; in this plight he is brought into the wedding house, frequently to the astonishment of strangers who are not in the secret, and begins to sing;
'O, I am a silly auld man,
My name is auld Glenae etc'
He is asked to drink, and by and by to dance, which after some uncouth excuses he is prevailed on to do, the fiddler playing the tune which here is commonly called Auld Glenae; in short, he is all the time so plied with liquor that he is understood to get intoxicated, and with all the gesticulations of an old drunken beggar, he dances and staggers until he falls on the floor, yet still in all his riot, nay in his rolling and tumbling on the floor, with some other drunken motion of his body, he beats time to the music, till at last he is supposed to be carried out dead drunk.' 88

The tune *'Auld Glenae'* was variously known as *'The Kirk wad let me be'*, *'The Blythsome Bridal'* and *'The Silly Old Man'*. It was a 9/8 or 6/8 jig. The dance was originally performed by two people, one to represent the sinner and the other the minister. When Burns described it the dance had lost its moral message and by the early part of the 19th Century had completely fallen out of use.

David Herd in his collection of Scots Songs preserves two of the verses of Auld Glenae or as he titles it "An the Kirk wad let me be';

'I am a poor silly auld man
And hirpling o'er a tree
Yet fain, fain kiss wad I
Gin the Kirk wad let me be.

Gin a' my duds were aff
And a' Hail claes on
O I could kiss a young lass
As weel as ony man.' 89

THE WOOING OF THE MAIDEN

Burns also witnessed another dramatic dance at a wedding in Nithsdale namely 'The wooing of the Maiden'. This combination of dance, recitation and pantomime was acted out by a boy and a girl dressed in antiquated costume. The theme of the dance was courtship and the vagaries thereof. The man goes astray but is brought to heel by the woman. Alan Cunningham in his Scots Songs gives a full account of this dance and also mentions a third dramatic dance of this type called *'The Rock and The Wee Pickle Tow'*. In this dance the woman with the rock and tow (distaff and flax) is pursued by the man with a lighted candle. The music started slowly, increasing in tempo as the chase developed. The woman twisting and turning to avoid the flame and preserve the tow. Inevitably the man succeeds in igniting the tow. Once again the symbolism of fertility arises and obviously this dance is about sexual intercourse. Fire being another fertility symbol. 90

BAB AT THE BOWSTER

As was the custom at every dance the last dance would be *'Bab at the Bowster'*. The title means in modern English - Dance at the Bolster or The Cushion Dance. The dance was conducted at the end of every convivial meeting, kirn, wedding or house heating. The dance was begun by one of the unmarried guests who taking a cushion in his hand, danced around the room; and at the end of the tune placed the cushion before one of the opposite sex who kneeling upon it was saluted by the dancer. The girl then took up the cushion,then both danced together. It was continued until all the company had shared in it. In essence the cushion was used as a go between, thus every male in the company had the opportunity to kiss every female as the dance went round.While the dance went on the following words were sung;

Company;
'Wha learned you tae dance
Babbity Bowster, Babbity Bowster
Wha learned you tae dance
Babbity Bowster, Brawly

Reply;
'My minnie learned me tae dance
Babbity Bowster, Babbity Bowster
My minnie learned me tae dance
Babbity Bowster Brawly
Company;
'Wha gie'd you the keys to keep etc
Reply;
'My minnie gie'd me the keys to keep etc
Company;
'Kneel doun, kiss the grun
Kiss the grun, kiss the grun
Kneel doun, kiss the grun
Kiss the bonnie wee lassie (laddie)

This last kissing would be accompanied with a squealing on the bagpipes or fiddle. 93
The symbolic connotation of this dance seems to be worship of the earth and the symbolic kissing of it showing respect and honour for the fertility and favour of the land on which depends human survival. One can only speculate as to the true antiquity of this dance but it first appears in the Skene Manuscript circa 1630 91 under the title *'who learned you to dance and a towdle'*, and appears in many later 18th and 19th century printed collections for both fiddle and bagpipes. Apart from a corrupted form as a childrens singing game the tune is seldom heard today, yet two centuries ago it was the most popular tune among the people. Robert Burns said of it *'This tune is to be met with everywhere'*. 92

Of course at intervals during all these dances bread and cheese, home brewed ale and hot punch would be served. While the young danced the older members of the assembly might seat themselves and drink and sing.

The Beddan

The beddan was the closing event. The bride would attempt to retire but as soon as she was missed there would be a general rush to the bridal chamber, which was burst open and filled in an instant to perform the ceremony of *'Beddin the Bride'*. After the bride was put in the bed a bottle of whisky and some bread and cheese was handed to her. She gave

each a dram and a piece of bread and cheese. Her left stocking was then taken off and she had to throw it over her left shoulder amongst the guests. It was then fought for by those in the room. Strong and long was the contest for it, as the one who remained the possessor of it was the first of that company who would be married. This practice must be the original of the bride throwing her bouquet to the young women when she leaves the reception.The bride had to sit up in bed until the bridegroom came and *'laid her doon'*. Sometimes the roughest of horseplay went on, it not being uncommon for the whole company getting on the bed with its resultant collapse. 94

The Kirkin

This however was not the end of the festivities. In certain districts marriage celebrations were continued for several days. In the 19th Century it was still common for the country folk to prolong the merrymaking and jollities from the day of the marriage to the close of the week. During this time the nuptial party made visits to the neighbours of their own rank and perambulated the district, accompanied by a piper and other mirthful attendants. 95

A *'kirkin'* took place on the Sunday following the wedding and was in early times attended by a large company but in later days there was often only three couples; that is the bride and groom, the best man and maid and *'anither lad an his lass'*. The party never under any circumstances took a bye-path to church, nor did they enter church until the service was well begun. After the service the party was entertained to a feast by the newly married pair. Such feasts were at times held in *'change houses'* where agood deal of drinking was carried out. Kirk Sessions at times tried to stop such practices. As in Cullen in 1785 ;

"It was observed by some members of the session that a practice prevailed in the parish of people meeting together in the publick houses upon the Lords day for what they called "Kirking Feasts' where they sat and drank and gave offence to their Christian neighbours'. 96

The kirkin was of course a public celebration of the consumation of the marriage. In the fishing communities of Fife it was the practice of the newly married women to wear a specially woven kirkin shawl.

Creelin

One last wedding custom is worth our notice and this was the *'creelin'*. On the first appearance of the newly married man at his work he had to *'pay-aff'* or stand his hand. Failing this he was creeled. In later days this consisted of beng rubbed over with dust or grime but in former times a creel or basket full of stones was bound on his back. If he has been a worthy husband and acted a manly part, his young wife cuts his cords with allacrity and relieves him of his burden. 97

This practice was also a test of manhood and affirmation of the consumation of the marriage.

'The De'il and St Andrew pairt ye!'

The Old Blacksmith's Shop Gretna Green.
Photo: G. Mooney

5—GRETNA GREEN
and other Scottish Marriage Houses

No account of weddings in Scotland would be complete without the story of Gretna Green. Gretna Green is famed the world over for its association with eloping couples and romantic weddings, but the reasons for its fame are less to do with Scotland and more to do with the formerly more onerous English Laws of marriage. Because of many abuses of marriage in England by bigamists and opportunists seducing young wealthy girls the Church and aristocratic establishment persuaded the Law Lords of England to formalise and control those *'irregular'* marriages which had become a booming trade particularly in Fleet Prison and surrounds.

Lord Hardwick's Marriage Act of 1754 made several new regulations. Amongst the most significant were that if a couple wished to marry they not only had to marry in Church, but also both had to be over 21 unless they had the consent of their parents.

Lord Hardwicks Act did not apply in Scotland where the legal age was (and still is) 16. A legal and binding marriage could be made in Scotland by declaring before two witnesses. The result, when theAct came into force, was the immediate flight of young lovers who wished to be married against their parents wishes to Scotland. And Gretna, along with Lamberton and Coldstream became the favoured locations for these quick marriages.

The best known of the various routes over the border between England and Scotland is to Gretna Green over the Rivers Esk and Sark. For centuries it has been famed as the way to Gretna Green and many a fine race between runaway couples and parents has been decided along this straight and almost level stretch of road.

Until 1940 couples could be married at a moments notice by the Smith at Gretna. Before that time Scottish law recognised as man and wife a couple who had made a plain declaration before witnesses and the age of consent in Scotland was 16. Since the Marriage Scotland Act 1940 it has been necessary for both parties to qualify by a residence of a least 15 clear days in Scotland before giving notice of intention to marry.

Originally the Gretna ceremonies took place in the village, but with the erection of a new toll bridge over the Sark, business was attracted to the toll house since it lay only a few yards over the Border and often only a few yards spelt the difference between marriage or not.

Marriages are still conducted at the Old Smithy and there is a visitor centre and a brisk tourist trade. Not only Gretna but Coldstream and

Lamberton were also noted as destinations for runaway marriages but it is Gretna which has capitalised on the romance of runaway marriages. Today it is a thriving business.

The Old Wedding House, Coldstream. — *Photo: B. Mooney*

Lamberton is just north of Berwick upon Tweed and once had a similar reputation among runaway couples as that of Gretna.
Coldstream bridge was built in 1763 and provided one of the principal crossing points into Scotland. The tollhouse at the north end of the bridge where many marriages were conducted can still be seen.
It is a remarkable fact that no fewer than three Lord Chancellors of England were married in this modest place . . . Lord Eldon, Erskine and Brougham.

A tune appears in Robert Riddells 'Collection of Scots Border and Gallovidian Melodies' entitled *'The English bring to Gratney Green the Lassies that hae siller'*. Apart from being one of the longest tune titles it gives a more realistic view of why certain men may have eloped with young women.

6—CONCLUSION

From the late 16th Century and throughout the 17th Century both the Church and Civil Authorities pressed restriction after restriction on penny bridals seemingly to no avail for they continued to be celebrated throughout the 18th Century and in the rural areas well into the 19th Century. The following accounts from the First Statistical Account of Scotland 1791-1799 testify to their resilience:

'A penny wedding is when the expense of the marriage entertainment is not defrayed by the young couple or their relatives but by a club among the guests.Two hundred people of both sexes will sometimes be convened on an occasion of this kind.' 3

'One, two and even three hundred would have convened on these occasions to make merry at their own expense for two or more days. This scene of feasting, drinking, dancing, wooing, fighting etc was always enjoyed with the highest relish.' 4

Some questions arise which deserve further examination. These are - why did the Reformed Church endeavour to place restraints on penny bridals and also why did the Civil authorities place restrictions on the celebrations?

It would appear that the motives of the Civil Authorities were economic. The first Act limiting penny weddings was made by Parliament in 1581 and Acts *'limiting the expense of marriages and banquets'* and similar enactments were made in 1621 and 1681.

The Act of 1681 stated that at bridals attendance be restricted to the immediate family and no more than *'four friends on either side, and their ordinary domestic servants'*.This Act also applied to baptisms and burials. The economic motives are revealed by the injunction: *'That neither bridegroom or bride, nor their parents or relations shall make above two changes of raiment that time or upon that occasion'*. 5

We noted previously how at Stirling and Kinneil the local authorities were concerned to control the demand for food and clothing to avoid imports and an excess of demand over supply, in line with the economic theories in fashion at that time.

The motives of the Church in restricting penny bridals seem more complex and require close examination.

At first direct action against bridals by the 16th Century Church Authorities is infrequent. Only where bridal celebrations impinged on the

Lord's day or where they involved extreme show of pomp and obvious consumption were Kirk Sessions outraged as at Edinburgh in 1574 where one Neil Laing was accused by the Kirk Sessions of *'making a pompous convoy and superflous banqueting'* at the marriage of Margaret Danielson, *'to the great slander of the Kirk'.* 10 and at Dalkeith in May 1594 ;

'The qlk day it was provided by ye presbyterie, in respect of the grait profanationg of ye Lords day be marriages, in pyping, fidling and dancing yat marriages suld be on ane oulk (week) day as also baptism ministerit provyding yat yr be ane day appoyntit, qr at yr ane resonabil congreation of pepil, yar preiching maybe maid.' 11

However attitudes gradually hardened and by the 1640's we see a new mood emerging and the first direct attacks on bridals being made by the Church Authorities. In February 1640 the Synod of Moray made the following decree:

'In respect of ye gryt disorders that haw fallen out in dyverse parts of ye land by drunkennes and tuilyeing (fighting) at pennie brydalls,...Thairfor it is ordained that thair be no pennie brythalls maid on ye Sabbathe'.

In October of the same year:

'Mr Johne Martiall (Minister of Duncros in the Synod of Moray) being found to have maid a marriage on the Thursday, and that the persones keipit a pennie brydaill on ye next Sabbath having a minstrell playing to ye church and from ye same befoir them, is sharplie and gravlie rebuked in ye face of ye Synod'. 12

At Elgin 24th June 1601;

'Alxander Thome and Agnes Pyerie find caution that sall not use fiddling, pyping, nor dancing nor any excess nor ryot nor yet come forth to the calsay under pains of 10 pounds and the parties to be married in the morn'. 13

At Dunkennard on 25th August 1631;

'In respect of the many abuses and disorders that falls out at penny brydalls, speciali of plays and drunkennes, it is ordained that no persone heirafter sall be maryed unles thai consigne pands that thai be no abuse at their brydell, under the painne of tenne pund'. 14

Breaking the Sabbath main crime but drunkenness, fighting and minstrels were also being frowned on. The underlying mood was put into words and action in 1645 when the General Assembly of The Church of Scotland issued the following Act;

'The General Assembly, considering the great profanitie and several abuses which usually fal forth at Penny Bridals, proving fruitful seminaries of all lasciviousness and debausherie, as well by the excessive numbers of people convened thereto, as to the extortion of them therein, and licentiousnesse thereat, ordain every Presbyterie in this Kingdom, to take such speciall care for restraining of these abuses, as they shall fit in their severall bounds respective.' 15

This Act was put into effect by Kirk Sessions in the years following. Some examples are as follows;
'The Presbyteries of Haddington and Dunbar declared that the paying of extravagant sums (1s Scots or 8d Sterling) caused; "great immoralities...piping and dancing before and after dinner or supper, drinking after dinner and so forth. Moreover loose speeches, singing of licentious songs and profane minstrelling in time of dinner or supper tends to great deboshery, through all which causes, penny brydalls in our judgement to become seminaries of all profanation. (They therefore ordained that no more than 20 people should ever gather on such occasions, and that all piping, dancing, singing and loose speeches should cease'. 16

At Glencros on 12th March 1646; *'The said day the brethern and ruling elders having taken to their consideration ye Acts of ye G'Real Assembly anent pennybrydles, likwaykes and that great abuses is at them, thought fit that at pennibrydles ther should only be 12 with the man and 12 with the woman - the price to be 12/- ye man and 8/- the woman, and the brekers of this whither on the persons to be mariet yr pairt, or the others there, to pay 10 pounds, qlk sum is to be consignit be the pairties before the day of mariage and yt there shall be no pypping wtout the house, or wtin after denner, nother drinking; under the forsaid penalties.'* 17
At Dumfries in July 1657 it was ruled that;
'..not more than 24 persones assemble at a wedding and that the expenses do not exceed 8 pounds and that under the payne of 20 pounds wherof the one half is to be payt by the bridegroom and the other half by the inkiepar whar the brydle is kept' 18

The Kirksession of St Cuthberts on 9th April 1646 ordained that under a penalty of 10 pounds couples should not invite to their weddings more than 24 persons. (Ref19) and at the Synod of Moray on 8th June 1675 the following Act was made;
'The qlk day the brethren of the sub-Synod convenied for the tym taking into thair grave and serious consideration the great disorders with the scandalous lacivious and unchristaine cariages of the comonalitie, for

the most pairt at pennie brydells, by thair frequent resort and great confluence ordinarilie at such occasions for removing of such evills and suppressing such disorders the Brethren foresaid thought fitt and expedient to constitut these following articles to be observed gravely in tym coming.
1.That the usuall excessive number to be limited and restricted to eight persons, on each side the maried persons.
2.That all piping, fidling and dancing with out doores of all whosoever resorting these meetings be restrained and discharged.
3.That all obsene, lacivious and promiscuous dancing within doores be discharged.
4.That the two dollars consigned at the contract of the married persons remaine in the Session Clarkes hands until the Lords day after the marriage, that in caise of contravening one or other of the foresaid two dollars shall be confiscated to the common good of the Parish Church, and this by and attour the publicke censur to be imposed upon the transgressors of the foresaid articles.

We can detect that the concern was not for religious observance but for '*the great profanitie and severall abuses*', namely '*lasciviousnesse, debausherie and licentiousnesse*', of secondary importance was the excessive numbers of people at bridals and the amounts they spent. Thus through all the controls we can see a direct attempt to control public morality and behaviour. The goings on at bridals had become unacceptable to the Elders and Session. A change had taken place in the establishment view of what was right and proper, and although censorship of the content of bridal celebrations might not have been possible censure of those taking part was.

Pipers in particular were subjected to stern punishments. The Kirk Session of Ashkirk ordained that:
'For pyping at bridels, Adam Moffat, pyper, on the next Sabbath to stand at the Kirk door with ane pair of sheittis (sheets) about him, beirfutt and beirlegitt; and after the pepill wes in, to go to the place of repentance,and so continue Sabbathlie induring their willis'. 21
And at St Andrews in 1658;
'Mure, pyper...diverse Brethren complained that Johne Mure pyper, is occasion of much disorder in ther congregations by his pypering at brythells and unseasonable drinkings.The said Johne compeiring, the Presbyterie discharged him to play at any brythells, or drunken lawings; with certification, if he be found to contravene he will be proceided against with the highest censure of the Kirk'. 22

Pipers became scapegoats because they were obvious targets and could be heard or caught in the act of inciting dancing. Perhaps by the public humiliation of pipers it was hoped to restrict dancing but what could be done about the *'loose speeches and singing of bawdy songs?'*
One thing is certain - none of these enactments or enforcements seems to have made little impression on putting a restraint on penny bridals. It seems that many were prepared to lose their consignation money and pipers were prepared to risk the stool of repentance to celebrate and enjoy weddings. Even elders of the kirk transgressed as this entry in the Kirksession of Hawick 1703 testifies.
'John Hart, elder, summoned for making a penny bryddall at his daughter Christians marriage which ended in scolding and fliteing. Hart was reminded that these meetings had been laid aside and were contrary to the Acts of Assembly and the laws of the Kingdom, whereupon he, upon his knees acknowledged his guilt ..and..prayer was made to God to grant him repentance and pardon for what he had done tending to revive the cursed custom of penny bryddells'. 22a

Penny bridals continued to be popular well into the 19th Century it was not civil or church laws which brought them to an end but profound social and economic changes which broke up the traditional communities and altered peoples aspirations. As material wealth increased the penny bridals became scorned and many were to say of them that *'they will not begin the world with begging'.*

The Penny Wedding — C. Lizars *National Gallery of Scotland*

NOTES ON THE SONGS AND MUSIC

THERE CAM A YOUNG MAN TO MY DADDIES DOOR

The words of this song are to be found in David Herd's, Ancient and Modern Scottish Songs, Vol II, p150, and the melody is from David Glens Collection of Highland Bagpipe Music, Part V. The tune is variously known as Lord Dunmores Jig and Bung Your Eye. Words and music probably both date from the mid 18th Century.

O WAT AND WEARY

The words given in the text are from David Herd's manuscript collection and they are a variant of the song collected by Robert Burns, known as *'Ay wakin O'*. The music given here is from the simpler set of the tune given in the Notes Illustrating Song No 213 in the Scots Musical Museum (p206 in the *'Illustrations'*).

I LOO'ED N'ER A LADDIE BUT ANE

David Herd included the words of this song in his Ancient and Modern Songs, Vol II, p338. The tune is clearly that known variously as *'My lodgings on the cold, cold ground'*, *'Believe me of those endearing young charms'*, and *'I loo'ed ne'er a lassie but ane'*. John Glen in his Early Scottish Melodies, p147 - 8 discusses whether the tune is Scottish or Irish but reaches no conclusion. The tune was first printed in 1775.

I HAE LAID THREE HERRING A SAUT

David Herd includes the fragment of this old song in his Ancient and Modern Scottish Songs, Vol II, p225. Burns re-united song with words in the Scots Musical Museum, Song 244. The tune first appeared in James Airds Selection of Scotch, English, Irish and Foreign Airs, Vol II, 1782. This is still a well known and played bagpipe tune.

JOCKEY SAID TO JENNY

The words of this song are found both in David Herds Collection, Vol II, p195 and the Scots Musical Museum, Song 61. The music is from the latter source. This song would seem to be of Border provenance being one of the 3/2 hornpipes mentioned by James Alan, the Duke of Northumberlands piper as being played *'Time out mind on the Border'*. I suspect that the tune and song date from at least the 17th Century and the song was first printed in Alan Ramsay's Tea Table Miscellany, 1724.

UP STAIRS, DOON STAIRS
The words of this song are given in David Herd's Collection, vol II, p181 and the tune noted is *'Jenny Dang the Weaver'*, which is still a well known reel tune of which both fiddle and pipe settings are to be found. The setting given here is from the Scots Musical Museum, Song 127. Bagpipe settings are very similar. The tune is very old and first appears in the Orpheus Caledonius 1733.

JENNY NETTLES
These words and music are from the Scots Musical Museum, Song 52 although the words also appear in David Herd's Collection. The tune first appears in Bremners Scots Reels etc, 1760 and seems to have been a popular dancing tune of that period.

THE FEET WASHING
This is most likely a 19th Century pipe jig and appears in David Glens Collection of Highland Bagpipe Music, Part XIV.

Pipers tunes for the Wedding Procession

There is still a vague tradition of playing certain tunes as the newly married couple leave church, if a piper is called upon to play. The usual tunes used today include *'The Keel Rowe'*, 'The *'Highland Wedding'*, and *'Highland Laddie'*. Some of these tunes are traditional but many of the tunes played in the past are now rarely used in the marriage context. Those mentioned in the text are:-

WOOED AN MARRIED AN A' (See notes on song later)
This pipers version is from David Glens Collection, Part XIV.

I HAE A WIFE O MY AIN (see notes on song later)
Setting from David Glen Collection, XIV.

HEY CA' THRU
This tune does not survive in the bagpipe tradition or in the printed pipe music collections but is never-the-less a pipe tune collected by Burns for inclusion in the Scots Musical Museum (see notes on song 392 later).

THE ROCK AND THE WEE PICKLE TOW
This is yet a popular pipe tune with a long pedigree. This setting is the one played traditionally in Linlithgow at the Riding of the Marches.

MERRY MAY THE KEEL ROWE
In Cromeks' 'Remains of Nithsdale and Galloway Songs', p125 he remarks that 'The Keel Row is a popular bridal tune in Scotland'. The old words to the tune also associate it with matrimony.

'Merry may the Keel Row, the Keel Row, the Keel Row,
Merry may the Keel Row, the Keel Row, the ship that my loves in.'

This reel version of the tune is from William Gunn's Collection of Pipe Music, 1860, where it is entitled *'The Bagpipe'*. The tune is very much a favourite of present day pipers.

Songs sung at the Bridal

THE BLYTHSOME BRIDAL
This 17th Century vernacular masterpiece was first printed in Watsons Choice Collection, 1709, and is found in the Scots Musical Museum and the Orpheus Caledonius. The Museum and Orpheus tunes differ and are both given below. The tune is not a pipe tune being better suited to the fiddle. The music is included in the Guthrie M.S.pre 1680, while the Orpheus version is the oldest printed form dating from 1725. The tune is variously known as *'Auld Glenae', 'The Silly Old Man'*, or *'An the Kirk wad let me be'*.

TO THE BEGGING WE WILL GO
This yet familiar song is to be found appropriately in Vagabond Songs and Ballads, where the following tune is given.

I GOTTEN THE LADDIE THAT I LIKED SAIR
These words come from a manuscript collection called the St Clair M.S., a collection of songs from the South West of Scotland. The melody which fits the words is *'The Campbells are coming'*, or as it is known in Northumberland *'Hexam Races'*.

I HAE A WIFE O MY AIN

I hae a wife o my ain
I'll be haddin tae naebody
I hae a pat and a pan
I'll borrow frae naebody

The title of this lively tune comes from the old song, a fragment of which is recorded by Wm Stenhouse in his Illustrations on the Scots Musical Museum. It was well known in the middle of the 18th Century but probably dates before then. Being in 9/8 time it gives grounds for belief that it is a Border jig. It goes well with *'Wooed an married an a'*. This version of the tune is from David Glens Collection, Part VI.

SOME SAY THAT KISSINGS A SIN

The words of this humourous song are found in David Herd's Collection, vol II. The tune he mentions is *'Auld Sir Symon'*, which is a very old pipe tune of English origin, first making an appearance in Playfords *'Recreation on the Lyra Viol'*, 1652. It also had popularity in Scotland during the 18th Century and survives as the childrens song *'Here we go loobie loo'*.

THE ROCK AND THE WEE PICKLE TOW

The words which I give here are from David Herds Collection, Vol II p92-93 and would seem to be the earliest and best which has survived. The version, given here is the oldest set of the tune which is to be found in Henry Playfords Collection of 1650.

I REDE YE BEWARE O' THE RIPPLES

The words of this old bawdy song are recorded for us by Robert Burns in his his Merry Muses of Caledonia. The melody given here is from John Glens Early Scottish Melodies. The tune appears in James Oswalds Caledonian Pocket Companion, Vol XI, 1759 as *'Beware of the Ripples'*. The ripples are the backache caused by too much sexual activity.

TAIL TODDLE

This well known reel tune has enduring popularity and dates from the 17th Century it occurs in Margaret Sinklers M.S. of 1710 and many other early 18th Century collections. William Stenhouse tells us in the *'Illustrations'* that this old tune was formerly called *'Fiddle Strings are dear laddie'* from the lines of an old song;

'Fiddle strings are dear laddie
Fiddle strings are dear laddie
An' ye break your fiddle strings
Ye'se get nae mair the year laddie'

At the end of the 18th Century it was probably better known as *'Tail Toddle'* from a bawdy song which had been a favourite among the country people. Robert Burns recorded this song for us in the Merry Muses of Caledonia.Tail Toddle is of course an euphemism for sexual intercourse.

THE REEL OF STUMPIE

The Reel of Stumpie was another favourite tune at penny weddings. Stumpie means much the same as in modern English, i.e. short and thick. *'The Reel of Stumpie'* is a facetious reference to the sexual act. The fertility aspect is appropriate to a wedding Robert Burns preserved the old song words which were sung to the tune in his Merry Muses. William Stenhouse tells us that this popular melody was known also as *'Jockey has gotten a wife'*. By the 19th Century the *'Reel Stumpie'* had become the rather longer *'Stumpie Strathspey'* versions of which are to be found in William Gunns Collection and David Glens Collection variously called *'Hit me gently with your tassles'*, *'Young Rory'* or *'The Highland Wedding'*. A simple change of time from 4/4 to 2/4 time and the well known march the *'Highland Wedding'* emerges out of the past to serve us in the present.

BROSE AND BUTTER

This popular bagpipe tune occurs in Lowland, Highland and Northumbrian traditions. In Northumberland it is known as *'The Peacock Followed The Hen'*, after an old childrens song (see Chambers-Popular rhymes). The setting I have used is a traditional one. Brose and Butter was popularly considered an aphrodisiac in pre-industrial society and explains the refrain in the song - the words of which are in Robert Burn's Merry Muses.

THE PLOUGHMAN

This song, full of double meanings, occurs in several collections mostly expurgated, however the most explicit is in the Merry Muses of Caledonia by Robert Burns. The accompanying melody is a simple yet attractive reel tune suited to the bagpipes. It was certainly in common use in the early 18th century and this setting is the one quoted in the Illustrations on the Scots Musical Museum, p158.

O WAT YE WHAT MY MINNIE DID

This humorous, witty and bawdy song is to be found in the Merry Muses. The tune given is *'How can I keep my maidenhead'*, which was also known as *'O Minnie'* and is included in Margaret Sinklers M.S.,1710. However another tune of the same name occurs in the Vickers Northumberland M.S. and this tune seems to suit the words better. For a complete discussion of *'O Minnie'* and the old tune see John Glen, Early Scottish Melodies, p138.

MY WIFES A WANTON WEE THING

This tune was first printed in Playfords, *'Original Scots Tunes'* 1700 as *'Brides Next'*. It takes its title from an old Scots song of the 17th Century. The song contains values which are opposite to those of modern day feminists but the song gives an insight into the lot of women in pre industrial society. Burns wrote a song based on the old words but with very different sentiments.

WOO'ED AN MARRIED AN A'

William Stenhouse, editor of the Notes Illustrating the Scots Musical Museum tells us that this humourous old song was omitted by Allan Ramsay in his Tea Table Miscellany, 1724, although it was quite current in the Border long before his time. The tune was originally a 9/8 jig and this version comes from David Glens Collection of Bagpipe Music, Part XIV. Today it is played as a 6/8 march considerably altered from the old tune. By no coincidence it is usually played with *'The Rock and the Wee Pickle Tow'* by todays pipers. The words are from David Herds Ancient and Modern Scots Songs, Vol II, p115.

HEY CA' THRU

This lively little bagpipe jig was preserved for us by Burns who included it in the Scots Musical Museum. It occurs no where else. The version of the words given here are from the St Clair M.S.

O FARE YE WEEL
THE MALTS ABOON THE MEAL THE NIGHT

This old song alluding to the problems of excessive drinking was included by David Herd included in his collection of Ancient and Modern Scots Songs, Vol II, p222. The tune is given in the Scots Musical Museum and is 'Alister' from Walshs Caledonian Country Dances, Book III.

CUTTYMUN AND TREELADLE

This excellent reel tune comes from the Pipers Assistant. It is closely related in style to Tail Toddle.

MAGGIE LAUDER

The tune mentioned in Paties Wedding was popular with pipers and fiddlers throughout the 18th and 19th centuries. Maggie Lauder was of course the heroine of a celebrated poem attributed to Sempill of Beltrees. A version of the of tune can be found in the Pipers Assistant.

BAB AT THE BOWSTER

This bagpipe version of the tune comes from Hendersons Tutor, 1891.

THE WOOING OF THE MAIDEN.

This tune is given in the Scots Musical Museum as the melody for *'Galloway Tam'*, song 325. In the Notes illustrating that song the following is stated; Burns says *'I have seen an interlude acted at a wedding to this tune called the 'Wooing of the Maiden'. These entertainments are now much worn out in this part of Scotland. Two are still retained in Nithsdale viz, 'Silly puir auld Glenlae', and this one.'* (Reliques). The air first appears in Oswalds Caledonian Pocket Companion, Book VI.

AN THE KIRK WAD LET ME BE

The lines of the old song *'Silly puir auld Glenlae'* appear in David Herds Ancient and Modern Scots Songs,Vol II, p224. See the Notes on *'The Blythsome Bridal'* for more on this melody.

JOHN GRUMLIE
This humorous song appears in Vagabond Songs and Ballads and is is noted as being a popular song at country weddings. It is derived from the older 16th Century poem (song) *'The Wife of Auchtermuchty'* which is to be found in the Bannantyne M.S.

JOHN ANDERSON MY JO
The old words of this song are recorded in the Merry Muses. The Andersons were hereditary town pipers of Kelso which explains the allusion to the *'chanter pipe'*. The earliest version of the tune is given by John Glen in his Early Scottish Melodies and is from Skene M.S. circa 1620.

THE COOPER OF DUNDEE
This is another song from the Merry Muses which I have re-united with its original melody *'Bonnie Dundee'* or *'Adieu Dundee'* which is given in John Glens Early Scottish Melodies, p45. The tune first appears in the Skene M.S. circa 1620.

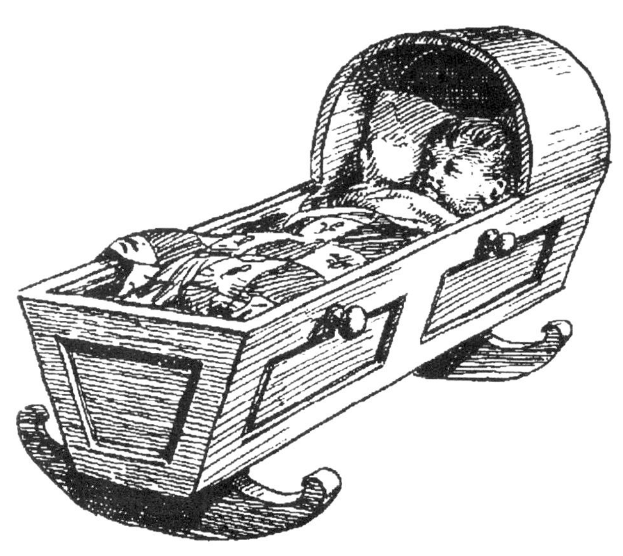

SONG WORDS

WOO'D AN MARRIED AN A'

Chorus
Woo'd an married an a'
Woo'd an married an a'
Was she nae very weel aff
Was woo'd an married an a

1.The bride came out of the byre
And O' as she dighted her cheeks
Sirs I'm to be married the night
And has neither blankets nor sheets
Has neither blankets nor sheets
Nor scarce a coverlet too
The bride that has a' to borrow
Has e'en right meikle ado

2. Out spake the brides father
As he came in frae the plough
O had ye're tongue,my doughter
And ye's get gear enough
The stirk that stands I' the tether
And our bra' bafin'd yade
Will carry ye hame your corn
What wad ye be at ye jad?

3. Out spake the brides mither
What devil needs a' this pride
I had nae a plack in my pouch
That night I was a bride
My gown was linsy-woolsy
And ne'er a sark ava
And ye hae ribbons and buskins
Mae than ane or twa.

4. What's the matter quo Willie
Tho' we be scant o claiths
Weel creep the nearer the gither
And we'll smore a' the fleas
Simmer is comin o
And we'll get teats o woo
And we'll get a lass o our ain
And she'll spin claithes anew.

5. Out spake the brides brither
As he came in wi the kye
Poor Willie had ne'er a taen ye
Had he kent ye as weel as I
For your baith proud and saucy
And no for a poor mans wife
Gin I canna get a better
I'll never tak ane I' my life.

6. Out spake the brides sister
As she came in frae the byre
O gin I were but married
Its a that I desire
But we poor folk maun live single
And do the best we can
I dinna care what I shou'd want
If I could get a man.

STUMPIE

My daddie was a fiddler fine
My minnie she made mantie O
And I myself a thumpin quean
An' try'd the reel of stumpie O

Chorus
Wap an row, wap an row
Wap an row the feetie o't
I thought I was a maiden fair
Till I heard the greetie o't

Lang Kail pease and leeks
They were at the kirstin o't
Lang lads wantin breeks
They were at the gettin o't

The Baillie he gaed farthest ben
Mess John was ripe and ready o't
But the sherra had a wanton fling
The sherra was the daddie o't

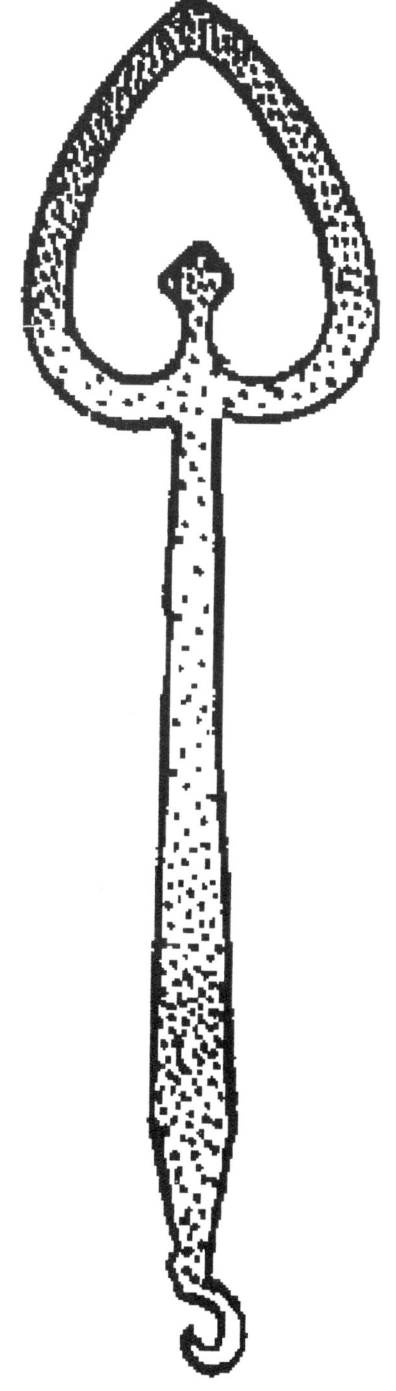

HEY CA THRO

Here's to the dance of Dysart
And the kimmers of Largo
And the brides of Buckhaven
And the gossips of Leven

Chorus
Hey ca thro, ca thro
For we hae muckle a do
And hey ca thro, ca thro
For we hae muckle a do

And Johnie Geordie rose
And he put on his clothes
When he bang'd up his trumps
The lasses came in by the lumps

And they had mutches and rails
And aprons wi peacock tails
And a sic busks sae bonnie
Come dance wi our son Johnnie

Maggie she kiss'd the piper
There could naebody wyte her
She had nae siller I trow
But she gae kisses anow

We have sheets to shape
And we have beds to make
And we have corn to shear
And we have bairns to bear.

TAIL TODLE

Our gudewife held o'er to Fife
For to buy a coal riddle
Lang or she came back again
Tammie gart my tail todle

Chorus
Tail Todle, Tail Todle
Tammie gart my tail todle
At my arse wi' diddle doddle
Tammie gart my tail toddle

When I'm dead, I'm out of date
When I'm sick, I'm fu o trouble
When I'm weel, I step about
An Tammie gars my tail todle

Jenny Jack she gae a plack
Helen Wallace gae a boddle
Quo the bride, its o'er little
For to mend a broken doddle

WAT YE WHAT MY MINNIE DID

O wat ye what my minnie did
My minnie did, my minnie did
O wat ye what my minnie did
My minnie did to me, Jo?

She pat me in a dark room
A dark room, a dark room
She pat me in a dark room
A styme I couldna see Jo

An there cam in a lang man
A meikle man a strang man
An there cam in a lang man
He might hae worried me, Jo

For he pou'd out a lang thing
A meikle thing, a strang thing
For he pou'd out a lang thing
Just like a stannin tree Jo

An I had but a wee thing
A little thing, a wee thing
An I had but a wee thing
Just like a needle e'e Jo

But an I had wanted that
Had wanted that, had wanted that
But an I had wanted that
He might hae sticket me Jo

For he shot in his lang thing
His meikle thing, his strang thing
For he shot in his lang thing
Into my needle e'e Jo

But had it no come out again
Come out again, come out again
But had it no come out again
It might hae stay'd for me, Jo

I REDE YE BEWARE O THE RIPPLES

I rede ye beware o the ripples, young man
I rede ye beware o the ripples, young man
Tho the saddle be saft, ye needna ride aft
For fear that the girdin beguile ye, young man

I rede ye beware o the ripples young man
I rede ye beware o the ripples young man
Tho music be pleasure, tak music in measure
Or ye may want win in your whistle young man

I rede ye beware o the ripples young man
I rede ye beware o the ripples young man
What'er ye bestow, do less than ye dow
The mair will be thought o your kindness young man

I rede ye beware o the ripples young man
I rede ye beware o the ripples young man
Gif you wad be strang and wish to live lang
Dance less wi your arse to the rafters young man.

THE MALTS ABOON THE MEAL THE NIGHT

And fare ye weel my auld wife
Sing bum be berry bum
Fare ye weel my auld wife
Sing bum, bum, bum.

Fare ye weel my auld wife
The steerer up o strunt and strife
The malts aboon the meal the night
Wi some, some, some.

And fare ye weel my pyke staff
Sing bum be berry bum
Fare ye weel my pyke staff
Sing bum, bum, bum

Fare ye weel my pyke staff
Wi you nae mair my wife I'll baff
The malts aboon the meal the night
Wi some, some, some.

THE COOPER O' DUNDEE

Ye coopers and hoopers attend to my ditty
I sing o a cooper who dwelt in Dundee
This young man he was baith amrous and witty
He pleas'd the fair maids wi the bunk o' his ee
He was nae a cooper, a common tub hooper
The most o his trade lay in pleasin the fair
He hoopt them, he coopt them, he bort them, he plugt them
An a' sent for Sandie when out o repair
For a twelvemonth or so this youth was respected
An he was as busie as weel he could be
But bisness increased so that some were neglected
Which ruined trade in the town o Dundee
A baillies fair daughter had wanted a coopin
An Sandie was sent for as oft time was he
He yerkt her sae hard that she sprung an end hoopin
Which banish'd poor Sandie frae bonny Dundee

JOHN ANDERSON MY JO

John Anderson, my Jo John
I wonder what ye mean
To lie sae lang i' the mornin
And sit sae late at e'en?

Ye'll bleer a your een, John
And why do ye so?
Come sooner to your bed at e'en
John Anderson, my Jo.

John Anderson, my Jo John,
When first that ye began
Ye had as good a tail-tree
As ony ither man;

But now its waxen wan, John
And wrinkles to and fro;
I've twa gae-ups for ae gae-down,
John Anderson, My Jo

I'm backit like a salmon
I'm breastit like a swan
My wame it is a down-cod
My middle ye may span;

Frae my tap-knot to my tae, John
I'm like the new fa'n snow;
And it's a for your convenience
John Anderson, My Jo.

O it is a fine thing
To keep out o'er the dyke
But its a meikle finer thing
To see your hurdies fyke, John
And hit the rising blow
Its then I like your chanter pipe
John Anderson, My Jo

When ye come on before John
See that ye do your best
When ye begin to haud me
See that ye grip me fast
See that ye grip me fast, John
Until that I cry, OH!
Your back shall crack or I do that
John Anderson, my Jo

John Anderson, My Jo John
Ye're welcome when ye please
It's either in the warm bed
Or else aboon the claes
Or ye shall hae the horns John
Upon your head to grow
And that's the cuckolds malison
John Anderson, my Jo.

THE ROCK AND THE WEE PICKLE TOW

There was an auld wife had a wee pickle tow
And she wad gae try the spinning o't
But louten her down, her rock took a low
And that was an ill beginning o't
She lap and she grat, she flet and she flang
She trow and she drew, she ringled she rang
She choaked, she boked, and cried let me hang
That ever I try'd the spinning o't

I hae been a wife these three score of years
And never did try the spinning o't;
But now I was sarked foul fa them that speirs
For it minds me o the beginning o't
The women now-a-days are turned sae braw
That ilk ane maun hae a sark, some maun hae twa,
But the world was better when feint ane ava
But a wee rag at the beginning o't.

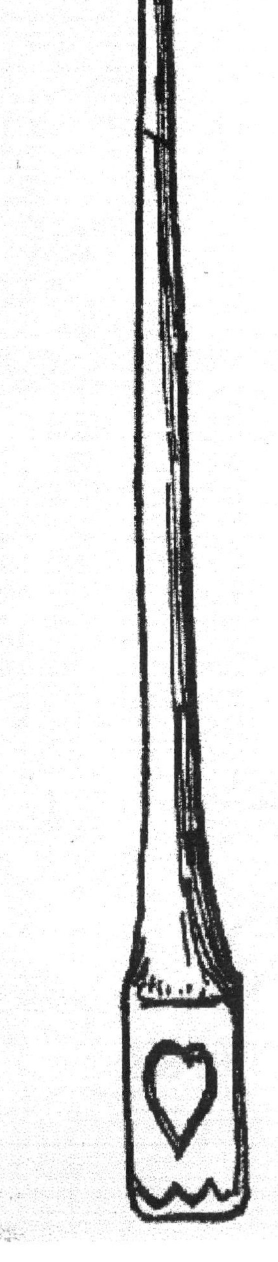

Foul fa' them that e'er advis'd me to spin
For it minds me o the beginning o't
I might well have ended as I had begun
And never had tried the spinning o't
But they say she's a wise wife wha kens her ain weird
I thought ance a day it wad never be speird
Now loot you the low, now tak the rock by the beard
Whan you gaed to try the spinning o't

The spinning, the spinning, it gars my heart sab
When I think on the beginning o't
I thought ance in a day to ave made a wab
And this was to ave been the beginning o't
But I had nine doughters as I hae but three
The safest and soundest advice I wad gie
That they frae spinning wad keep their hands free
For fear o an ill beginning o't

But in spite of my counsel if they wad needs run
The dreary sad task o the spinning o't
Let them seek out a loun place at the heat o the sun
Syne venture on the beginning o't
For, O do as I've done alake and vow
To busk up a rock at the cheek of a low
They'd say that I had little wit in my pow
And as little I've done wi the spinning o't

JOHN GRUMLIE

John Grumlie swore by the light o the moon
And the green leaves on the tree
That he could do mair wark in a day
Than his wife could do in three
His wife rose up in the mornin
Wi cares and troubles enou'
"John Grumlie bide at hame John
And I'll gae haud the plough".

Chorus

Sing fal-de-lal-lal, de lal-lal
fal-lal-lal-lal la-loo-oo

John Grumlie bide at hame John
And I'll gae haud the plough
First ye maun dress your children fair
And put them a in their gear
And ye maun turn the maut, John
Or else ye'll spoil the beer
And ye maun reel the tweel John
That I span yesterday
And ye maun ca in the hens, John
Else they'll a lay away

Oh he did dress his children fair
And put them a in their gear
But he forgot to turn the maut
And so he spoiled the beer

And he sang aloud as he reel'd the tweel
That his wife span yesterday
But he forgot to ca in the hens
And the hens a laid away

The hawket crummie loot doon nae milk
He kirned, nor butter gat
And a gaed wrang, and noucht gaed right
He danced wi rage and grat
Then up he ran to the head of the knowe
Wi mony a wave and shout
She heard him as she heard him not
And steer'd the stots about

John Grumlies wife cam hame at e'en
And laughed as she'd been mad
When she saw the house in siccan a plight
And John sae glum and sad
Quoth he,"I'll gie up housewife-skep,
I'll be nae mair guidwife".
"Indeed", quoth she, "I'm weel content,
Ye may keep it the rest o your life."

"The deil be in that", quoth surly John
"I'll do as I've dune before".
Wi that the gudewife took up a stout rung
And John made aff to the door
"Stop, Stop, gudewife, I'll had my tongue
I ken I'm sair to blame
But henceforth I maun mind the plough
And ye maun bide at hame

CUTTYS WEDDING

Busk and go, dearie go
Busk and go to Cutty's wedding
Busk and go, dearie go
Busk and go to Cutty's wedding

Cutty is a bonny lad
And he has a little wifie
He'll gae to the town his lain
When she taks ony fickie fykie

Daddy says he winnae gae
Mammie says she was nae bidden
I'll put on my ruffled cuffs
And slide awa to Cuttys wedding.

MY WIFES A WANTON WEE THING

My wife's a wanton wee thing
My wife's a wanton wee thing
My wife's a wanton wee thing
She winna be guided by me

She played the loon ere she was marry'd
She played the loon ere she was marry'd
She play'd the loon ere she was marry'd
She'll do't again ere she die.

She sell'd her gown and she drank it
She sell'd her gown and she drank it
She row'd hersell in a blanket
She winna be guided by me

She did it although I forbade her
She did it although I forbade her
I took a rung and I claw'd her
And a braw gude bairn was she

There cam a young man tae my Daddies Door *Song Air*

The Rock and the Wee Pickle Tow *Song Air*
(1678 Playford)

The Rock and the Wee Pickle Tow *March/ Jig*

I loo'ed na' a laddie but ane — *Song Air*

Woo'ed an' married an' a' — *Jig*

Jockey said to Jenny — *Hornpipe*

Jenny Nettles

Song Air

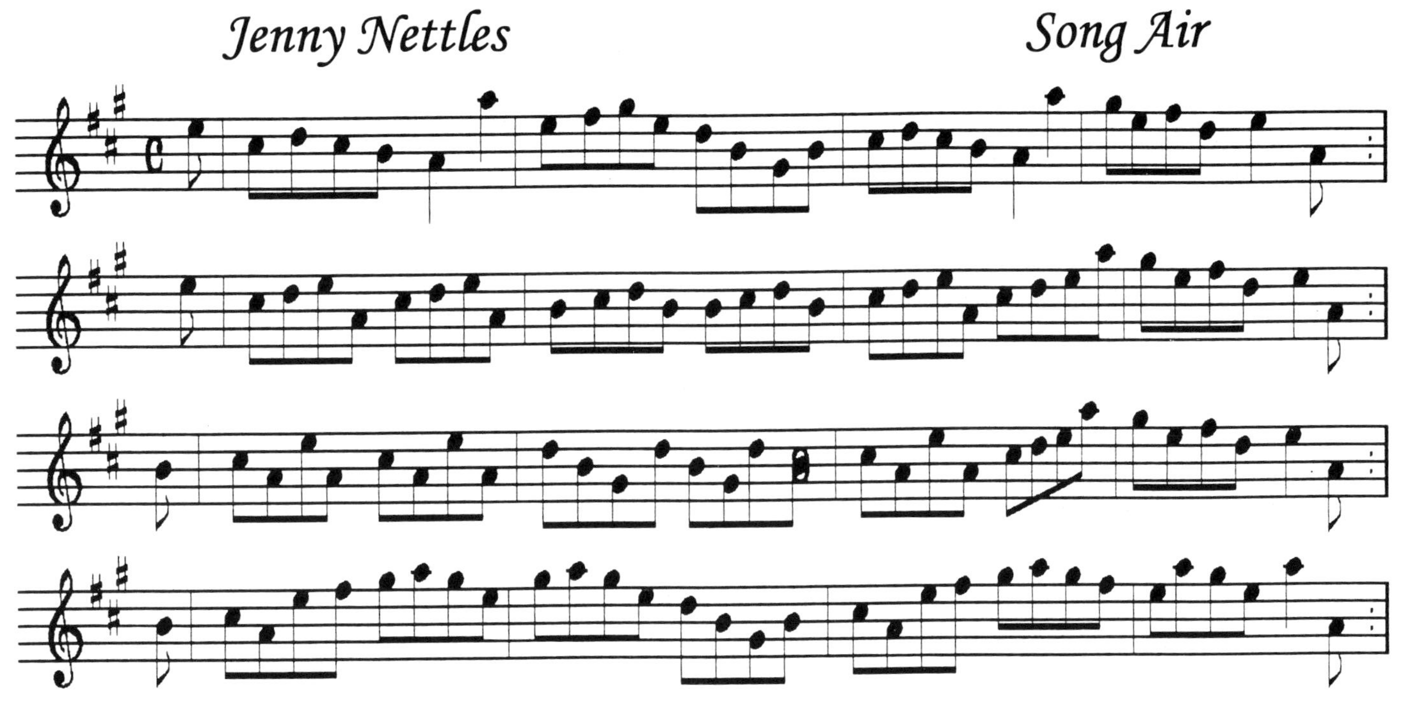

The English bring to Gratney Green the Lassies.

Song Air

Would the Minister not Dance — *Jig*

Brose and Butter — *Jig*

The Feet Washing — *Jig*

A beggin' we will go

Song Air

O' Fare Ye Weel

Song Air

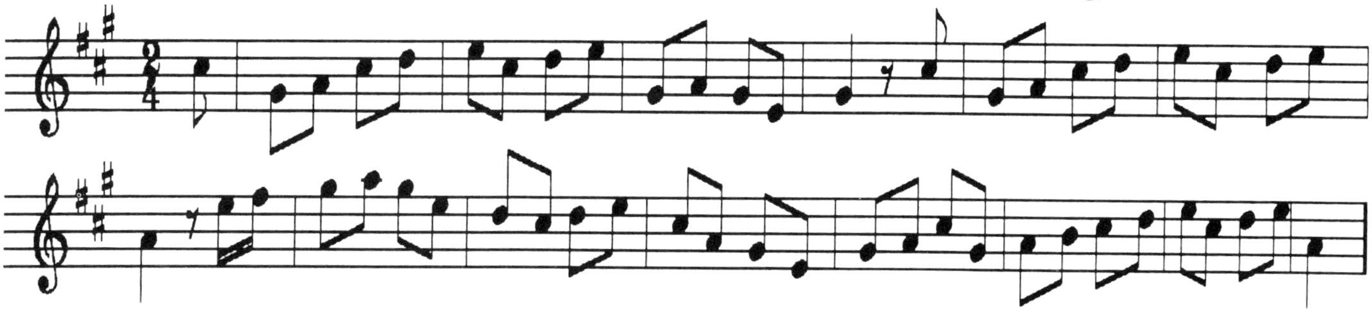

Jenny Dang the Weaver

Song Air/ Reel

Hey Ca' Thru

Jig

I Rede Ye Beware o' the Ripples — *Song Air*

The Ploughman — *Song Air*

The Blythsome Bridal — *Song Air*

Aye Wakin O' — *Song Air*

Bab at the Bowster   Jig

I gotten the laddie that I liked sair   Song Air

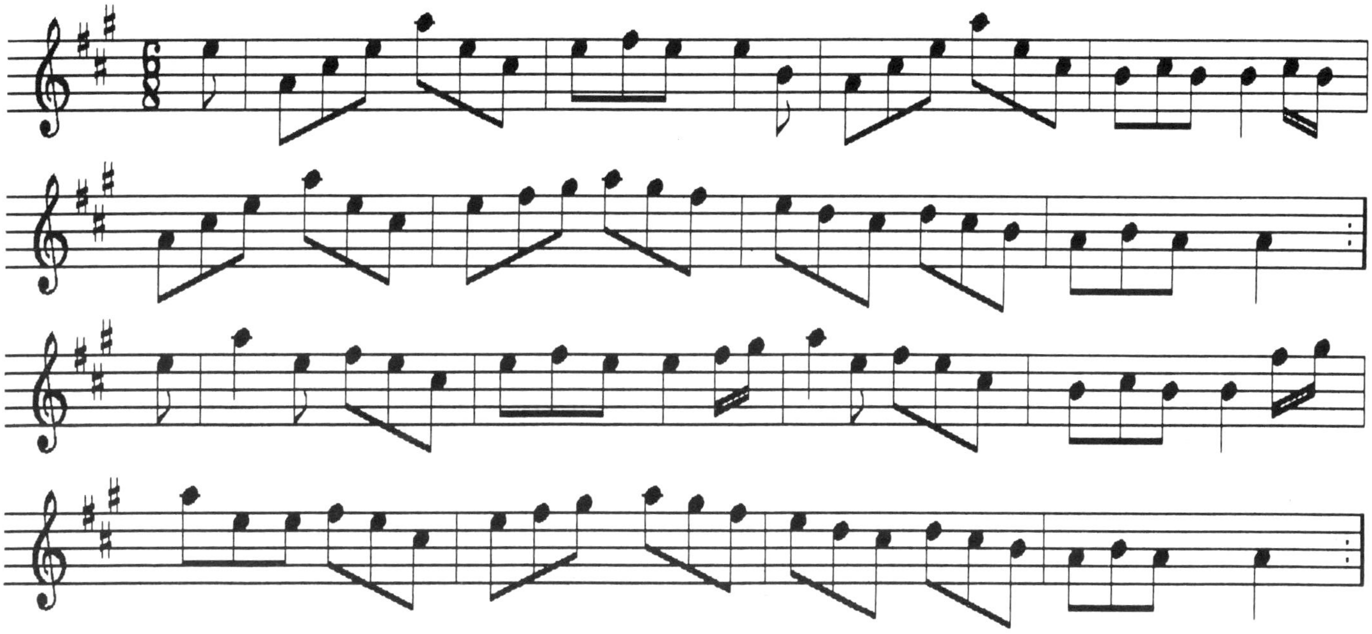

The Cooper o' Dundee   Song Air

The Reel of Stumpie or

Reel

Jockey has gotten a wife or Buttered Peas or
Hit me gently with your tassels or Wap an' Row the Feetie o' it

How can I keep my maidenhead?

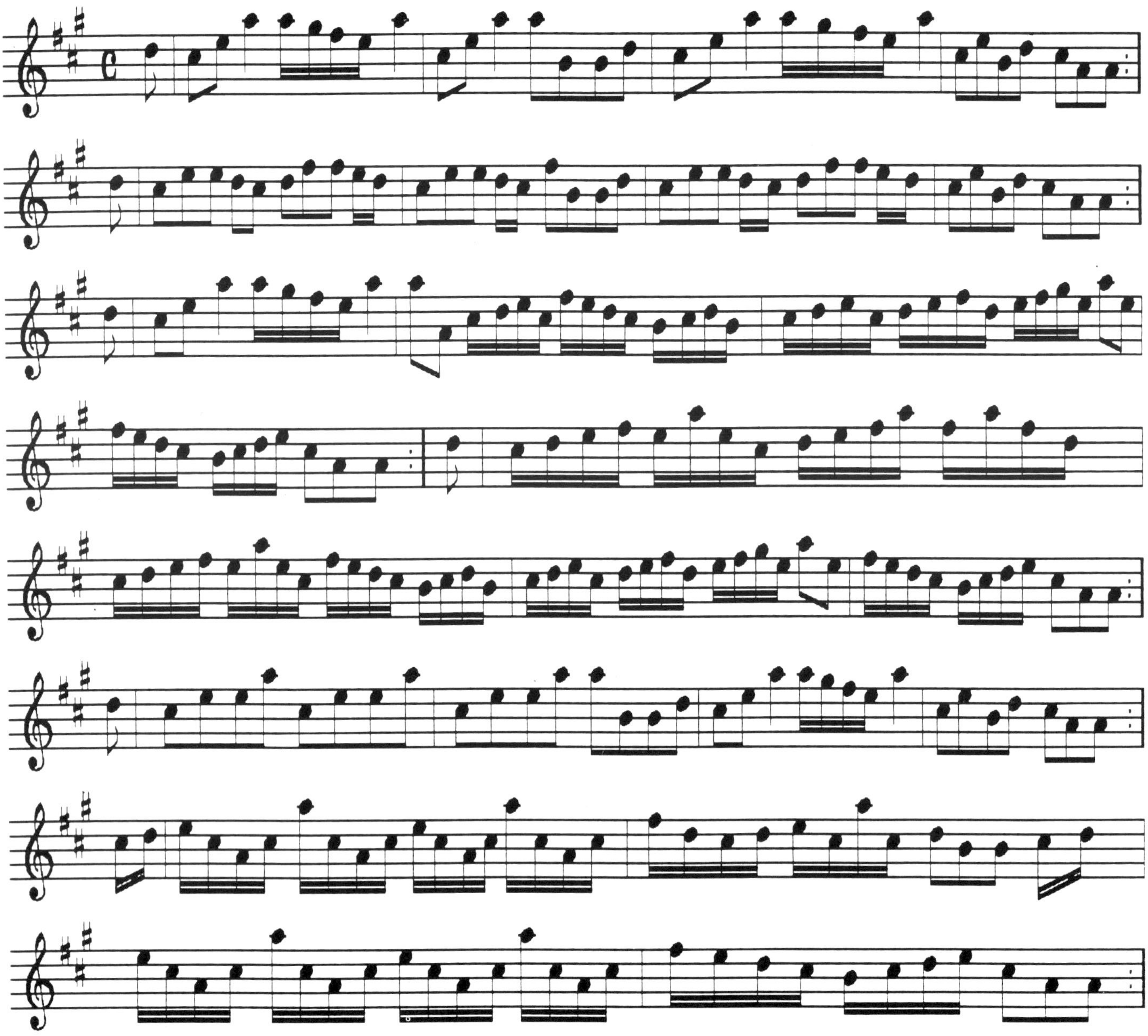

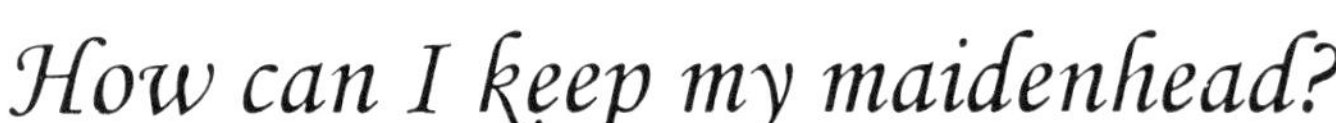

Song Air

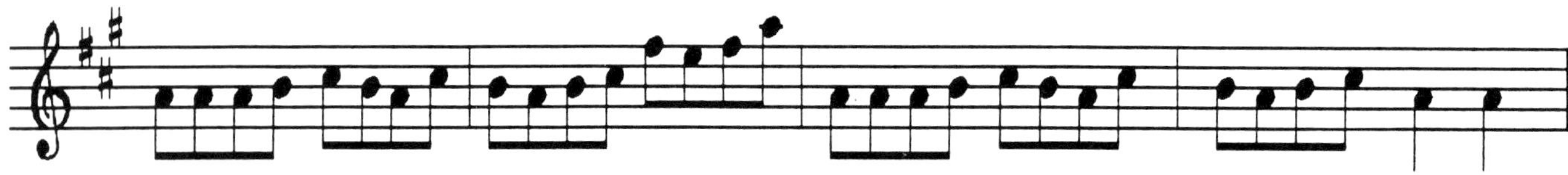

I hae a wife o' my ain — *Song Air /Jig*

Auld Sir Symon — *Song Air*

Maggie Lauder — *Song Tune*

Cuttymun and Treeladle

Reel

Tail Toddle

Reel

My Wife's a Wanton Wee Thing

Song Air

Merry May the Keel Row — Song Air / Reel

The Blythsome Bridal

Woo'ed an' Married an' a' — Bagpipe set

REFERENCES

1. Extracts from Stirling Burgh Records 1680, Vol 2, p30, Glasgow, 1887.
2. Regality Court Book of Kinneil, 8 Feb 1672. In Borrowstounness and District, T.J.Salmon, Edinburgh, 1913, p92-93
3. Parish of Drainy - First Statistical Account of Scotland 1791-1799, vol IV, p86, Edinburgh
4. Parish of Montquhitter - First Statistical Account of Scotland, vol XXI, p146, Edinburgh.
5. History of Civilisation in Scotland, J.Mackintosh, vol 3 p280-281, Paisley, 1892-96
6. Worship of Scottish Reformed Church 1550-1638, W.McMillan, London 1930, p266-281
7. Scottish Historical Review Vol XXXVII, p89-17, A.E.Anton ,re Handfasting
8. Worship of the Scottish Reformed Church, p267
9. Quoted in 7 above
10. Social Life in Scotland, Rev Rogers, Edinburgh, 1884, p123
11. Extracts from Presbytery Book of Strathbogie p4, Spalding Club, Aberdeen ,1843
12. Synod of Moray, 1640, History of Moray and Nairn
13. Elgin, 1601, History of Moray and Nairn
14. Dunkennard 1631, History of Moray and Nairn
15. Act of General Assembly 1645 - in Scots National Dictionary under Penny Bridal
16. Presbyteries of Haddington and Dunbar 1647 - Chambers Domestic Annals, Vol2, p162, Edinburgh 1874
17. Glencrose, 12 March 1646, Extracts from the records of the Presbytery of Dalkeith, 1582-1848
18. Dumfries July 1657 - Social Life in Scotland, p122
19. St Cuthberts Kirk Session 9 April 1646 - Social Life in Scotland, p122
20. Act of Synod of Moray 8th June 1675 - History of Moray and Nairn
21. Kirk Session of Ashkirk - Social Life in Scotland, p123
22. St Andrews Kirk Session 1658 - Social Life in Scotland, p123
23. County Folklore, Vol VII-Fife, London 1914,Appendix p39
24. Notes on the folklore of the North East of Scotland, Rev W.Gregor, London 1881
25. Notes on the Folklore of the NE
26. Ancient and Modern Scottish Songs, David Herd, volume II p150, Scottish Academic Press, Edinburgh and London 1973
27. Ancient and Modern Scottish Songs, Vol II, p226
28. Songs from D.Herd Manuscript Hans Hecht, Edinburgh, p10
29. D Herd Collection vol II p338
30. The Letters of Robert Burns, edited by Francis Allen, London, 1917
31. D Herd Collection, vol ii, p225
32. Scots Musical Museum, Song 61
33. Bannatyne M.S. 1568
34. D.Herd Collection ,vol II, p181
35. Jenny Nettles Herd, p60, vol ii
36. Primitive Beliefs in N.E.Scotland-J.M.McPherson, London, 1929, p118-123
37. Primitive Beliefs
38. Notes on the Folklore of N E Scotland Rev W Gregor London 1881, p81-101
39. Traditional Number Rhymes and Games, F.D.Gullen, London, 1950
40. County Folklore, Notes on Folklore of the North East of Scotland
41. Primitive Beliefs in N.E. Scotland
42. Primitive Beliefs
43. Notes on Folklore
44. Chambers Scots Dictionary
45. Notes on Folklore
46. Notes on Folklore
47. Notes on Folklore
48. Notes on Folklore
49. Notes on Folklore
50. Notes on Folklore
51 Biggar and the House of Fleming, W.Hunter Edinburgh 1867,p328-329
52. N.E Folklore
53. County Folklore Vol VII Fife-London, 1914, Appendix, D.Rorie M.D. p392
54. Quoted in Primitive Beliefs (Henderson,Banchory/Devenick 246f)
55. County Folklore, Vol VII, p392